D1070843

STUDIES IN ENGLISH LITERATURE

Volume IX

SHAKESPEARE'S EARLY COMEDIES

A Structural Analysis

by

BLAZE ODELL BONAZZA

La Habra, Calif.

1966

MOUTON & CO.

LONDON · THE HAGUE · PARIS

LIBRARY OF CONGRESS CATALOG CARD NUMBER: 65-28169

Printed in The Netherlands by Mouton & Co., Printers, The Hague

43,973

TO AEROL ARNOLD,
WHO PROVIDED THE ORIGINAL IMPETUS
FOR THIS STUDY

TABLE OF CONTENTS

INTRODUCTION

The purpose of this study of Shakespeare's early comedies has been to follow the steps in his progress from tentative experimentation to full competence in the craft of fashioning popular dramatic entertainment for an Elizabethan audience. The investigative procedure followed has been an inductive one based on a close reading of the plays themselves with attention being directed to dating, sources, textual problems, and topical allusions only to the extent that these matters might help illuminate obscurities relating to the playwright's development as a master craftsman of dramatic structure. By the term "structure" is meant not simply plot mechanics, although this is clearly central to a study of structure, but the whole fabric of the play: the incidents and their design, the use of characterization to further plot, the use of language to create character and tone, and the use of language and setting to create a motivating atmosphere. The play was conceived of as being ideally an "organic" unity in which all the parts play an indispensable role in maintaining the "life" of the total organism.

It is hoped that this structural analysis will lead to certain advantages that other methods of study might not provide. By studying all the elements of a play and their interaction, it might be possible to gain a greater degree of insight into Shakespeare's methods and their evolution and come to a fairer appraisal of his accomplishments as a dramatist. First of all, it might lead to a better understanding of the mechanics of the play – why certain things are done at a certain time, why characters are drawn as they are, why the particular setting is chosen. Secondly, it might provide criteria to determine how effectively he has combined the various elements or indicate where he has fallen short. Thirdly, it might illuminate the "meaning" of Shakespearean comedy since, if there is such "meaning", it probably resides in the entire structure of the play rather than in any of its fragments.

Attention has been confined here to the earlier comedies with the expectation that a pattern of development would show itself and a final, perfected scheme would become inducible. It is assumed here that Shakespeare did not start out as a fully competent dramatist – that he had to learn this difficult craft gradually, first by tinkering with old plays and collaborating with others. Not until he had worked with the problems of stagecraft as an apprentice did he undertake the fashioning of plays of his own contriving; even then he still relied heavily on imitation. He was still not certain of the path to follow because he had not yet evolved his own concept of the comic and perfected the stage techniques to realize it. He evolved this concept only by working it out in the course of several highly derivative plays in which he tried to master the practical matters of stage techniques, of entrances and exits, of setting up his situation, of initiating complications and conflict, of building suspense to lead to a climactic action, and of unraveling the tangled skein of action he had wound together. It was this process of working his way through these early efforts, of making mistakes and learning from them that made it possible for this highly gifted young poet to learn the difficult art of stagecraft just as Marlowe, endowed with similar gifts, had struggled to learn it but had died before he completely mastered it. Admittedly, these first comedies of Shakespeare, with the exception of *A Midsummer Night's Dream*, are far from the degree of excellence of the best of his later ones. What is primarily held for them is that they show the stages in his progress, uneven as it is, and anticipate the structure of his mature successes in romantic comedy.

In this process of evolving a comic concept and developing technical skill, he experimented with the linear, farcical comedy of the Plautine pattern but found it too uninvolved and uni-tonal to have more than a limited appeal for his heterogeneous audience. He worked with the comedy of Lyly and found that its affectations of language and absence of dramatic intensity weakened its appeal for a popular audience but that its subplot technique was something that could be used and developed with profit to overcome the flatness of the Plautine structure. From this point on he had to learn to add the elements of romance and complexity of story as Greene had shown could be done. This he attempted in *The Two Gentlemen of Verona* but discovered that he had to solve the problem of atmosphere before he could successfully combine romance and comedy. He solved this combination of problems brilliantly in *A Midsummer Night's Dream*. Here Shakespeare used the changes of identity of Plautine comedy, the elegance and beauty of language of court comedy, the parodying subplot of Lyly, and the complicated romantic plot of the Sidney-Greene school of romance rendered acceptable on the stage by an agreeable dramatic climate of his own devising.

The procedure followed in the handling of the first three plays has been to consider initially matters of dating, sources, textual problems, and topical allusions as they relate to the chronology of the plays, the raw material of the story, the theme the playwright was attempting to handle dramatically, and the type of audience he was trying to appeal to since these are all matters that might conceivably influence the analysis of the structure of the play. Once this preliminary evidence has been examined and evaluated, the play itself has been studied in terms of exposition, plot levels and connections, complications and intrigues, ironic reversals of intentions, of roles, and of fortune, comic catastrophe and denouement, characterization, language, tone, and atmosphere. The study of the fourth selection, *A Midsummer Night's Dream*, departs from the method of inquiry used with the three earlier plays. Here the study has been conducted on a more theoretical and less minutely detailed plane with the intention of summarizing what has gone before, inducing general principles, and formulating predictive criteria. This concluding section also attempts to evaluate the earlier plays in the light of the accomplishments of this finished work of dramatic art.

The results of this study would seem to support the thesis that the development of the structure of Shakespearean romantic comedy can be traced, as was originally hoped, through an analysis of the four early comedies: *The Comedy of Errors, Love's Labour's Lost, The Two Gentlemen of Verona*, and *A Midsummer Night's Dream*. This last play is seen as representing the first successful fusion of the structural elements the playwright had experimented with earlier: the use of comic reversals in a complicated, multi-level plot, the characterization of opposing and balancing elements, the employment of contrasting tones, and the creation of a motivating atmosphere influencing the plot and contributing to the thematic unity of the play through the use of appropriate language.

The Comedy of Errors is primarily concerned with the mechanics of plot, especially the manipulation and multiplication of ironic reversals. The main agencies of plot propulsion are seen to be a motivating circumstance outside the main action and the liberal use of accident and coincidence within the main action. Although characterization is elementary, there is an attempt to create the romantic heroine in the person of Luciana, Adriana's sister. The central farcical tone connected with the events involving the sets of twins is contrasted with a tone of pathos by wrapping the main incidents in a serious enveloping action involving the plight of Aegeon, the old father of the twins, thereby giving significance to the denouement beyond that of simple comic *anagnorisis*. In this attempt to master comic reversals and to balance contrasting tones, beauty of language is neglected except for a few felicitous touches, and characterization is stereotyped and rudimentary.

In *Love's Labour's Lost*, the main action, revolving around the absurd compact and its failure, is counterbalanced by a parodying subplot having its own ironic reversals and relating to the climactic reversal in the main plot. Basically, however, action and the development of dramatic suspense are sacrificed to a brilliance of language which does little to assist in the forward movement and complication of incident, with the result that the ironic reversals are episodic and only weakly climactic.

The Two Gentlemen of Verona presents a complex plot involving a chain of related complications that lead to multiple intrigues and derivative ironic reversals. Motivation for the ironic reversals comes about primarily through physical movement rather than through any impetus provided by functional characterization or appropriate atmosphere. The success in complicating the main action is offset by static exposition, an anti-comic atmosphere, and inadequate use of characterization to help bring about a dramatically effective resolution. The clowns in the subplot are not used for much more than total contrast; they are never given an independent line of action which balances the main plot and contributes to a total thematic effect.

In *A Midsummer Night's Dream* the problem of comic structure is solved. The play operates on four levels of action, each level being integrated with and balanced against the others. Exposition is handled economically and swiftly, comic conflicts are set up early, and the appropriate characterization and atmosphere is created to propel the action forward through a series of incidents of continuing and augmenting comic suspense. These incidents lead to a climactic reversal followed by an inevitable comic catastrophe and a convincingly motivated resolution. The enveloping action is used not merely as a framework but also to initiate the main action, help complicate it, absorb it when resolved, and furnish tonal contrast. The subplots are related to the enveloping action, to the main action, and to one another; they work harmoniously through character, incident, and tone to create a composite effect.

Thus, as a result of what he had learned from the writing of the three earlier comedies, Shakespeare was able to write a skilfully integrated multi-level, tonally contrasting romantic comedy, *A Midsummer Night's Dream*. This play, operating through the evolved structure it represents, brings about a state of balance from contrasting elements within the various plots, character groupings, and tonal complexes. All this is accomplished through the media of repeated ironic reversals arranged climactically, motivated by both circumstance and character, and sustained by an appropriate atmosphere effected through the power of language. All that is left to be done in the playwright's later successes in romantic comedy is to elevate the romantic heroine to full equality and thereby bring the love interest to the fore: a Julia must be converted into a Rosalind, a Rosaline into a Beatrice, and a Luciana into a Viola. Some explanation of the symbols and special terms used in the analysis of the four plays is needed here. In the solution that Shakespeare finally reached in *A Midsummer Night's Dream*, the multi-level, tonally contrasting plot structure is seen to consist of four parts. These parts or separate plots are represented in this study by the letters A, B, C, and D according to their temporal existence and function in relation to the entire play.

The A plot is the enveloping action or framework of the entire play. It may appear first or be delayed, but it always concerns circumstances and events that are antecedent to those of the B plot and determinative of them. In *The Comedy of Errors* and *A Midsummer Night's Dream*, it appears first; in *Love's Labour's Lost* it appears later than the B plot; in *The Two Gentlemen* it is absorbed into the B plot. The primary function of the A plot is to initiate the first movement and complication in the B plot and eventually absorb the B plot once it is resolved.

The B plot, or romantic love story, has its events set within the framework of the A plot. It is motivated and resolved by events arising within the other plots and by characterization within its own structure. It is related to the A and D plots primarily by incident and to the C plot by tonal contrast. In *The Comedy of Errors* and *Love's Labour's Lost* it is set in motion and resolved by the A plot and tonally contrasted with the C plot. In *The Two Gentlemen* it is resolved by an imperfectly developed D plot and in *A Midsummer Night's Dream* by a fully developed one, and, in both, tonally contrasted with the C plot.

The C plot, or parodying subplot, is used as an agency to incorporate the clowns Elizabethan audiences loved and also to provide tonal contrast to the B plot. In *A Midsummer Night's Dream* it is also used to help resolve the conflict within the D plot.

The D plot, or atmosphere-providing plot, operates primarily as a moving and complicating force, but it also has its own internal conflict which is resolved through its interaction with one of the other plots. In *A Midsummer Night's Dream* the D plot of Oberon versus Titania is resolved by its contact with the C plot of the Athenian mechanicals. The atmosphere the D plot provides makes possible the incidents in the love story, and its internal action serves as a counter-theme to that of the enveloping plot.

Since all these elements do not appear together in a fully developed form until *A Midsummer Night's Dream*, the analysis to follow will often involve pointing out how the absence of one or more elements affects the structure of the particular play being considered. The formula does apply in detail to the last play considered in this study, and, it is hoped, may provide structural criteria for the study of the later romantic comedies. The formula will be used here to determine the stages in Shakespeare's progress as a comic dramatist from early experimentation to a finished pattern of execution in the fashioning of romantic comedy.

I. *THE COMEDY OF ERRORS*

The Comedy of Errors is generally considered to be one of Shakespeare's earliest plays, and by some to be the earliest of his comedies. A play called *A Comedy of Errors* ("like to Plautus his Menaechmus") is recorded in the *Gesta Grayorum* as having been acted by a group of players, "a company of base and common fellows", at Gray's Inn as part of the Christmas revels on December 28, 1594. There is no reason to doubt that this play was Shakespeare's *The Comedy of Errors*.

Although all the evidence, both external and internal, indicates that this is an early play, there is some controversy over the exact year of composition. The doggerel in III.i and elsewhere in the play has been adduced as proof that the play represented a revision of an earlier work, perhaps the lost *The historie of Error* played at Paul's in 1577, or *A historie of fferrar* played by Sussex's men in 1583.[1] This revision theory has not won much credence, and it is generally believed this is Shakespeare's own play, written somewhere around 1591 or 1592.

Recently the probable date of composition of 1591-92 has been under attack. Sidney Thomas argues that the play could have been written as late as 1594 and that the Gray's Inn performance could have been the first one ever given. This desire to postdate the play is based on a strong admiration for the professional competence of the playwright. Thomas feels that it is incredible that Shake-

---

[1] Geoffrey Bullough, *Narrative and Dramatic Sources of Shakespeare*, I (London, 1957), p. 3.

speare could have begun his career with so skilful and adroit a play.[2]

Regardless of the uncertainty over the exact year of composition of the play, there should be little question about the playwright's possession of a high degree of professional competence. A structural analysis of the play shows that the dramatist arranges his comic situations skillfully so that they lead up to a climactic effect. Allardyce Nicoll feels that at first glance one might be tempted to pass the play with only an indulgent comment – that it is merely a farce with no direct bearing on the later comedies – but that a closer examination will show that it clearly outlines the greater comedies of the future.[3]

Although this play uses only two elements of the A-B-C-D plot structure and, then, not in a multi-level fashion, it does exhibit a relation with the later, finished structure that first appears in *A Midsummer Night's Dream* in its use of tonal contrast. Shakespeare achieves this through the use of an enveloping action, or plot A, which contrasts a pathetic note with the farcical tone of the comedy of errors of the B plot. This may seem a trivial movement in the direction of the full tonally contrasting, multi-level formula, but it is an essential part of the pattern that develops later. Contrast in tones is as important an element as coterminous action in the fully evolved A-B-C-D pattern. In this early effort Shakespeare uses this important device of combining tones, thereby creating a harmonious blend instead of the single note he found in his sources.

The plot of the comic action of the play comes from the *Menaechmi* of Plautus, which was in turn probably a redaction of a lost Greek comedy. The rather lengthy prologue tells of an old merchant of Syracuse whose wife gave birth to twin sons so much alike that not even their nurse could tell them apart. When the boys were about seven years old, the father took one of them with him on a trading journey to Tarentum in southern Italy. The little boy strayed away in the bustling market place and was kidnapped by a rich merchant of Ephesus who took him home with

---

[2] "The Date of *The Comedy of Errors*", *Shakespeare Quarterly*, Autumn, 1956, pp. 376-384.
[3] *Shakespeare: An Introduction* (New York, 1952), p. 68.

him and made him his adopted son. The dejected father died shortly thereafter and the grandfather renamed the remaining twin Menaechmus after himself and the lost brother. In the meantime, the kidnapped boy grew up in Ephesus the son of a wealthy merchant, had a wife and dowry chosen for him, and inherited a substantial fortune and social position on the death of his foster father. Meanwhile Sosicles, now named Menaechmus also, grew up in his native Syracuse. When he came of age, he set out in company with his slave, Messenio, in search for his long-lost brother.

The play proper opens in Epidamnus and the audience is introduced successively to Peniculus ("sponge"), a gluttonous parasite; Menaechmus I, a wayward husband; Erotium ("little love"), the courtesan and mistress to Menaechmus I; Cylindrus ("rolling-pin"), the courtesan's cook; Menaechmus II and Messenio, his slave; Erotium's maid; Mulier ("wife"), Menaechmus' wife; Senex ("old man"), her father; and Medicus ("doctor").

The action begins with Menaechmus' disclosure to the parasite that he is planning a dinner rendezvous for them both at the home of his mistress, the courtesan, for whom he has stolen one of his wife's best dresses by wearing it under his own cloak. When Menaechmus I and Peniculus leave to pass the time until dinner drinking at a nearby wine shop, Menaechmus of Syracuse, who has just arrived in the city, accompanied by his slave, comes on the scene and is mistaken for his twin by Cylindrus, the courtesan's cook, and invited to dinner. In spite of his slave's warning that the city is a notorious hot-bed of thieves and swindlers, he accepts the invitation and dines with his brother's mistress. While there, he is given the stolen gown to be altered and a gold bracelet to be repaired, both of which items he plans to appropriate as his own, intending to outwit what he considers to be a band of clever scoundrels and thieves. From the moment Cylindrus mistakes Sosicles for Menaechmus confusion triumphs, and while Sosicles enjoys the best of everything, Menaechmus is beset with a plague of misfortunes. He is betrayed to his nagging wife by the spiteful parasite disappointed in his gluttony, locked out by both his wife and mistress, declared insane by a quack physician, and finally rescued only by the timely arrival of Messenio, who effects a *cognitio* or recognition in a rather prolonged question-and-answer session in which the common parentage of the two Menaechmi is revealed and the confusion resolved.

As the above résumé of the plot would indicate, the tone of the Roman play is completely boisterous and gross, and the cleverly contrived actions completely selfish.

It is a realistic tale about the doings of certain commonplace people of rather low morals and is strongly marked by the conventions of Roman social life. The men appropriate what they can lay their hands on; the wife has no rights, and there is not even a suggestion, except from her own clamorous tongue, that she is entitled to any; the slave, a clever chap, is beaten; there is a parasite who has attached himself to Menaechmus the Citizen and is something of a blackmailer, and there is a courtesan of characteristic greed and conventional respectability.[4]

Menaechmus of Syracuse is as crafty and scheming as his Epidamnian counterpart. He has no scruples whatsoever about stealing or misrepresenting as long as his actions meet with success. He is motivated chiefly by the self-seeking desire of the Levant merchant to cheat in anticipation of being cheated.

The other characters are equally coarse and repellent. They are interesting not in themselves but only as types. Mulier is the customary strident-voiced shrew; Peniculus is the conventional unscrupulous parasite motivated solely by greed and spite. The courtesan is the materialistic, grasping female representative of her profession; the father is the stereotyped comically ineffectual *senex iratus*; the doctor, the usual quack anxious to render the diagnosis necessary to earn a quick fee.

This facile, stock characterization is to be expected since Plautus' play makes no pretence of being anything other than pure farce, i.e., that type of comedy in which the action is unrelated to character or stems from characters so superficial or stereotyped that they are not engaged in any genuinely voluntary activity but are at the mercy of events, mostly coincidental. Since the heart of the action depends on the absence of dissimilarities between the Menaechmi, no attempt is made to delineate character differences by thought, word, or action. We have human identity reduced to the lowest possible

---

[4]   Hardin Craig, *An Interpretation of Shakespeare* (New York, 1948), p. 21.

level, that of physical appearance, and we must assume that human beings are somewhat less than human – they must have some of the features of automata, as Bergson suggests, in order for farce to succeed. They must be manipulatable and incapable of exercising truly rational judgment.

Since farce is situation-centered and the characters are primarily manipulatable puppets, there is no real focus of attention on the action of any one or two individuals. It is the state of confusion resulting from the improbable and extravagant action that attracts our attention and we find it difficult to identify with the weakly drawn characters. We do not care so much about what happens to a particular character as we do about the resolution of the absurd situation.

Along with the improbability and extravagance, the rapidity of the action affects our ability to identify with the characters. Many of Plautus' scenes are so short as to allow only an entrance, a few words, and then a hasty exit. Act V, for example, has nine scenes: Menaechmus II and Mulier appear in scene i; Mulier and Senex appear in scene ii along with Menaechmus II; Senex alone in iii; Senex and Medicus in iv; Menaechmus I with Senex and Medicus in v; Messenio in vi all by himself; Senex, slaves, Messenio, and Menaechmus I in vii; Menaechmus and Messenio in viii; Messenio and the two Menaechmi in ix. It is evident that this rapid shifting from one character to the other minimizes individuals and emphasizes situation.

But pure farce is not interested in delineating subtleties of character; its sole aim is to excite laughter, laughter of the raucous variety – "the non-reflective guffaw". This laughter is excited by the ridiculous situation always verging on violence or coarseness. It insists that we accept the impossible as possible and silliness as a happy substitute for sense. It neither ridicules as does satire or burlesque nor exposes the well-spring of human emotions as does true comedy. It rests content if it leaves the viewer gasping for breath and holding his sides, spent from laughter.

Shakespeare attempts to shift the emphasis from situation to character by setting the mechanical elements of farce within a larger, more humane framework and by trying to create more subtle characters. He begins his play with a scene, probably borrowed from the story of Apollonius of Tyre found in Gower or Twine, in which Aegeon, an elderly merchant of Syracuse, pathetically explains his presence in Ephesus. He tells the Duke, who has condemned him to death as a merchant from a hostile city, that some twenty-five years previously his wife had given birth to twin sons while they were in Epidemnus. As attendants for his own sons he had bought the twin sons of a poor woman lodging in the same inn. On their return voyage, their ship had been sunk in a violent storm. He had managed to save one son and one infant slave by lashing them and himself to a spar, and his wife had done likewise with herself and the other two infants. He and his charges were rescued and taken to Epidaurus; his wife and the other two infants were picked up at sea and carried away by a Corinthian fishing boat. When the son rescued with the father reached eighteen, he left Syracuse, with his father's permission and in company with his slave, to search for his brother. Hearing no word from his son for two anxious years, the old man wandered about for five years more in vain search for his lost family. His quest had brought him to Ephesus and to his death sentence because of the trade war. After hearing this woeful tale, the Duke grants the old man a day to raise the ransom money to purchase his freedom.

Antipholus of Syracuse, the old man's son, has also just arrived n Ephesus with his slave, Dromio. The youth is unaware of his father's presence in the city and of the presence of his long-lost brother for whom he has been fruitlessly searching for seven years. He sends his slave to an inn with their money and, while along, is summoned by his brother's identical slave to come home to dinner. He becomes angered at what he believes to be an ill-timed practical joke and gives the slave a sound drubbing.

The physically chastized and thoroughly confused Dromio returns home complaining of the beating and here he is further upbraided by his impatient mistress for the annoying delay at the dinner table. In the meantime, the Syracusian Dromio, on his return from the inn, is beaten for denying he had invited his master to dine with a supposed wife. Adriana, the wife of Antipholus of Ephesus, and her sister, Luciana, come in search of the presumed husband and virtually brow-beat him and his slave into accompanying them home.

During the mismated dinner, the real husband and his dinner companions are denied entrance and ordered away. The angry husband decides to dine at the courtesan's and asks Angelo, the goldsmith, to bring along a gold chain which he had intended as a gift for his wife but which he now plans to give to the courtesan instead. Inside the house, Antipholus of Syracuse is attempting to woo the perplexed sister and Dromio is being amorously pursued by the ugly kitchen maid. Angelo returns from his shop, finds the wrong Antipholus at the house, and forces the gold chain upon him.

Angelo, encountering a merchant who demands instant payment for a debt owing to him, goes in search of Antipholus of Ephesus and requests payment for the gold chain of the dumfounded citizen. Payment is naturally refused and Antipholus is arrested on Angelo's complaint to the accompanying officer. At this moment the wrong slave appears and he is sent for bail money. Meanwhile the courtesan comes upon the twin in possession of the gold chain and she demands it in payment for a ring she had given the other Antipholus at dinner. When she is rudely denied, she seeks out Adriana claiming that Antipholus is deranged. When Dromio of Ephesus returns with a rope he had been sent for earlier instead of with the bail money the other Dromio had gone after, he receives another beating.

Adriana, Luciana, the courtesan, and Pinch, who has been retained to exorcise the demons in possession of the presumably demented Antipholus, now come on the scene. The enraged citizen and his slave are seized and taken away bound and restrained by Pinch and servants. When the other Antipholus and Dromio appear on the scene immediately thereafter with swords drawn, Adriana and Luciana run off in fear, believing that the violently raging husband and slave have escaped their guards and are intent on doing them mischief.

Angelo reappears and confronts the Antipholus who has possession of the chain and accuses him of bald deceit and misrepresentation. Adriana and Luciana reappear and the frightened master and slave, suspecting them of sorcery, seek sanctuary in a nearby priory. The abbess of the priory refuses to deliver the refugees over to their pursuers and Adriana appeals to the Duke, who is passing by with Aegeon and others on the way to the place of execution. The Ephesian master and slave now come on the scene and appeal for redress of grievances. There is considerable confusion based on statement and counterstatement until the abbess appears with the Syracusans. The recognition leads to a joyous reunion, the liberation of the unfortunate Aegeon, and the suggestion of the impending nuptials of Antipholus of Syracuse and Luciana.

A comparison of the plot summaries discloses that Shakespeare has divided the dramatic emphasis between situation and story, with the latter receiving less emphasis. The classical play had revolved entirely about situation and incident and the tone was hard and cynical, the series of callous chicaneries of the various characters being capped by Sosicles' suggestion to Menaechmus that he abandon his wife, sell his possessions, and accompany him to Syracuse. By placing the events of the prologue within the play itself, as had already been done in Italian versions such as *I Simillimi* of Trissino and *La Moglie* of Cecchi, Shakespeare is following the tendency of medieval romance to tell a story from the very beginning to the end and, by so doing, he also changes the tone from the coarse to the pathetic. The playwright, even in a work derived primarily from classical sources, refuses to be cramped by the restraint imposed by the Greco-Roman stage conventions: instead of being confined into the one form of complicated situation resolving, he chooses to follow the involved story line of romance. As Muriel Bradbrook says:

Thus in this early work we can already seen the pattern of Shakespearean comedy evolving, i.e., the amalgamation of incident with romance or story tinged with the marvelous. Here the full story

He was confronted with the alternatives of Italian tradition, with all its prestige and its ready models, or the shapeless native popular play, in which material designed for narrative was struggling to accommodate itself to dramatic form.[5]

[5] *The Growth and Structure of Elizabethan Comedy* (London, 1955), p. 77.

for its own sake is incorporated into the dramatic situation, made part of it, and made to bear on the central incidents within the play. It is easy to notice how the strong influence of romance, as seen in the element borrowed from Apollonius of Tyre, has swept aside all limitations of the classical dramatic form. Now there is no longer any obstacle to the intermingling of comic and tragic tones.

In Plautus all of the action in the play is contained within a single plot with the beginning of the story being relegated to a tongue-in-cheek prologue and the ending dismissed with a flippant proposal. In Shakespeare four separate but related plots, i.e., the arrest, scheduled execution, and salvation of Aegeon; the mis-understandings and resolution of the mistaken identities; the estrangement by jealousy and the reconciliation by love of the husband and wife; and the wooing and winning of Luciana, are interwoven into a single main plot. The peril and release of Aegeon is at the core of the serious action; it impinges on the comic action, resolves it, and is resolved in turn by it. The jealousy of Adriana leads to the estrangement from her husband and this in turn contributes to the complications of the comic action. The resolu-tion of the comic action leads to a happy culmination of the embryonic love plot involving Antipholus of Syracuse and Luciana. The various elements of the plot are not all adequately developed and the pattern remains relatively simple, but the effort shows the future bent of the playwright's mind and offers promise of a later harmonious complexity of plot construction.

This attempt at a harmonious complexity of plot construction can best be seen by a structural analysis of the various incidents within the play, disclosing their relationship to one another and to the entire play. In the first scene the playwright is concerned with laying the groundwork of the enveloping or serious action, i.e., the pathetic plight of Aegeon, and to indicate the basis of the internal or comic action, i.e., the mistaken identities. This two-fold objective is accomplished through a slender trial scene consisting mostly of exposition and stage setting for the final dual resolution. Aegeon is the first to speak and the audience is immediately informed that he is being sentenced to death. Since this is a comedy, the audience by convention realizes and expects that somehow this threatened execution will be averted no matter how inevitable it might seem on first acquaintance with the situation. The audience takes it for granted that the dramatist will sow the seeds of the eventual solution to the problem in the first scene. By doing so, the playwright provides his audience with the pleasure of anticipating how the happy resolution can be effected.

The Duke's first words inform us that Aegeon is a merchant of Syracuse hence subject to death for being apprehended in Ephesus. The existence of a trade war sets the necessity of the harsh penalty and exonerates the Duke of the charge of tyrannical cruelty. Northrup Frye points out how common it is for the action of a Shakespearean comedy to begin with some absurd, cruel, or irrational law which the action of the comedy then evades or breaks.[6] The Duke is here represented as being reluctantly forced to carry out the stern mandate even though by nature he is a merciful man. In this way the mood appropriate to the breaking of the law is established. Any pathos that might still be built up, however, is allayed by his saying,

> Again, if any Syracusian born
> Come to the bay of Ephesus, he dies,
> His goods confiscate to the Duke's dispose,
> Unless a thousand marks be levied,
> To quit the penalty and to ransom him.   (I.i.19-23)

The audience is secure in the belief that somehow the fine will be paid and the unfortunate old man rescued from death.

The next thing for the playwright to establish is when and how this will happen. With Aegeon's words, "My woes end likewise with the evening sun" (I.i.28), the audience is made aware of the time limitations that will govern the ensuing action. With lines 29 ff. the Duke by interrogating the condemned man establishes the "how" of the happy resolution. His gratuitous questioning provides the entré for a long expository section which has no legal bearing on the trial or the penalty but which is dramatically necessary to

---

[6] *The Anatomy of Criticism* (Princeton, 1959), p. 166.

set the stage for the internal action and to prepare the audience for the comedy of errors arising from the improbable existence of two sets of identical twins whose destinies are closely woven together. Aegeon obliges with a fully detailed account of the motivating circumstances lying behind his coming to Ephesus. He has come in search of his two long lost sons" ... the one so like the other / As could not be distinguished but by names". Here the dramatist is guilty of carelessness in a significant detail. From this remark we are led to assume that the twins were given different names; yet when we meet them in the play, we find they have the same name. For the mistaken identities in the internal action to occur, identical names are necessary and the playwright forgets to provide for this detail. Plautus had solved this simply by mentioning the renaming of one twin after his brother was lost. Shakespeare forgets to do so, but in the hustle-and-bustle of the comic action the omission is overlooked. The main purpose of this portion of the exposition is, of course, to convince the audience that since not even the parents could tell the children apart, all kinds of confusion can be expected to result from this remarkable similarity.

Furthermore, the birth of another set of twins in the same inn on the same night that Aegeon's sons are born forewarns the audience to suspend the laws of probability for the sake of entertainment and to be willing to expect all sorts of coincidences based on the original one.

Under the semblance of dramatic dialogue between the Duke and the overwrought Aegeon, the long expository speech of the latter is momentarily interrupted. This is done both for the benefit of the audience and of the actor playing the part of the old man. The one would become bored and restless with too long an uninterrupted account; the other would have difficulty remembering such a lengthy tale without some cue or change of tack. Later on Shakespeare learns to handle his exposition more adroitly but here he is still a relative novice. Aegeon goes on to tell of the motivating circumstances behind the entire play, i.e., the storm at sea, the conventional shipwreck, the rescue, and separation. The Duke is an exhaustive prober – all for the benefit of the audience. The dramatist uses him as a stalking-horse to elicit the full details of the enveloping action and to provide the material for the credibility of the forthcoming internal action.

Of the total 159 lines in the scene, 104 are spoken by Aegeon. The Duke's remarks are only to elicit background material of the doomed man's life, to provide further exposition of his own, and to prefigure the solution to the execution complication in the alternative which he offers. On the surface, this alternative seems tantamount to another death penalty since the prisoner is a stranger in an alien land. But the audience has been rendered receptive to coincidence and, knowing of the existence of the twin sons, is prepared for the old man's liberation and happy reunion with his family. When the Duke says,

> Therefore, merchant, I'll limit thee this day
> To seek thy life by beneficial help.
> Try all the friends thou hast in Ephesus;
> Beg thou, or borrow, to make up the sum
> And live; if no, then thou art doom'd to die.
>
> (I.i. 151-55)

the audience is assured that justice will somehow be tempered with mercy. It realizes that as a stranger Aegeon has no friends in Ephesus and if he is to be saved, as surely he must be since this is a comedy, he must encounter his wandering son, the long-lost son, his wife, or most happily and most likely all of them. Since all of them escaped death in the shipwreck, reunion is demanded by convention. The playwright's task is to bring about this reunion but it must not be done too soon or the tension building possibilities will come to nothing. The inevitable must be postponed until the internal action has been drained of its last comic possibility. When this occurs, the internal action will terminate in a juncture with the enveloping action centered about Aegeon's plight and impending execution at sunset.

Antipholus of Syracuse and his Dromio are the first to be introduced in the internal action of the play. Their presence affords an immediate opportunity to tie the enveloping action in with the internal action. Here the audience sees the twin the father had reared until he had left in search of his brother some seven years previously. To forestall the question of why he too is not apprehended as an enemy alien, the playwright uses the device of having the First Merchant warn him of Aegeon's fate and of the necessity for pretending to be from Epidamnum rather than from the hostile city of Syracuse. In this speech the merchant also serves to establish the time for the audience once again, i.e., the action must take place in the course of a single day, for the doomed Aegeon "Dies ere the weary sun set in the west" (I.ii. 7).

With Antipholus of Syracuse's first speech the internal action is set into motion. To provide the audience with its first view of one of the pairs of twins, Dromio of Syracuse must be sent from the stage on some pretext or other so that his double can appear and the audience thus see Aegeon's account of identical twins come to life before its eyes. To effect this necessary departure Dromio is given specific instructions, "and stay there, Dromio, till I come to thee" (I.ii.10). This serves as a signal to the audience: by this caution it knows that any Dromio reappearing shortly on the stage will be the twin from Ephesus. Antipholus provides himself with an excuse to "view the manners of the town" thus permitting occasion to develop whereby he will be mistaken for his counterpart. The audience is required to accept the stipulation that the two masters never meet throughout the internal action. Coincidence is to operate only to bring master and slave together, never master and master or slave and slave. On Dromio's departure his master remarks on his trustworthiness and his tendency to practical joking. This rather unsubtle bit of characterization is introduced to prepare for the credibility of the later confusion of identities. At this point it is important that the First Merchant be provided with an excuse to leave the stage, otherwise he would be present to testify to the true identity of Antipholus of Syracuse and the comic conflict would not materialize. In a sense, the comic hero must be isolated to meet his fate.

In Antipholus' short soliloquy, "I to the world am like a drop of water / That in the ocean seeks another drop", the audience is informed through irony and metaphor that its expectations will be realized, that this one drop of water will meet its counterpart as unlikely as it may seem on the surface. In fact, this is the theme of the entire comedy: strange and comical events will transpire once unrestrained coincidence has its sway, but eventually all will turn out well.

When Dromio reappears on the scene after specific instructions to stay at the inn until joined by his master, the audience realizes, although Antipholus does not, that this is the other slave that Aegeon spoke of. The audience, by benefit of the lengthy exposition in scene i, knows more than does Antipholus of Syracuse; therefore, it can accept this coincidence, in fact take pleasure in anticipating it. Dromio's remarks are interpreted as an ill-timed jest in accordance with Antipholus' previous analysis of the slave's character with its tendency toward "merry jesting". The audience, being wiser than either participant in the action, sees the confusion inherent in the situation and takes delight in the comic possibilities. That a master should be annoyed at the supposed intransigence of a slave he never gave orders to involves a dual reversal of intention. He intends to reprimand a recalcitrant slave in order to secure obedience and respect, but instead he scolds a tractable one and receives resentment and anger. Dromio intends to summon his master to dinner, but instead invites a total stranger.

With this scene the pattern of the comic action is established: the characters in their attempts to act in accordance with commonsense will experience repeated reversals of intention and of fortune. Repetition will be the keynote of the comic action. Not just one or two but all of the characters will experience one or more reversals. The playwright will utilize his *donné*, the physical repetition of individuals, of master and slave, to produce repetition of incident. The audience has seen the first reversal of intention in the slave's invitation to the wrong master and the first reversal of fortune in the beating he receives. It can now anticipate a series of similar comic reversals, comic because of their repetitiveness and also because of their intrinsic variance from commonsense expectations. Although the basic element is the repetition of reversals, this principle of action must obviously be used with variations. These can be achieved by a shifting of scenes and characters so that the force of the original improbability draws all the characters into a widening circle of involvement. The audience as the arbiter of commonsense is moved to laughter by the thwarted anticipations and annoying frustrations of the characters as they undergo the various reversals. Laughter results from the fact that the violation of commonsense expectations leads not to disaster but only to temporary discomfiture and distress.

The mention of the sum of money entrusted to Dromio serves a two-fold purpose. It is the cause of the comic misunderstanding between the master and the wrong slave, and it also serves to remind the audience of the enveloping action. It recalls the fact that the condemned man needed a thousand marks to procure his freedom and now it is seen that his son is present in the same city with exactly that sum of money on hand. With these two facts at its disposal, the audience is furnished with the clues necessary for it to anticipate a happy conclusion to the enveloping action it witnessed in scene i. In the meantime, however, it looks forward to being entertained by the complications promised by the internal action.

The act ends with Antipholus of Syracuse providing himself with an explanation for this confusing occurrence involving his slave's recalcitrance: he interprets it as an indication that witchcraft is rampant in this evil city, a notion that Shakespeare may have taken from Acts XIX which tells of St. Paul's missionary visits to Ephesus.[7] This explanation is important to the action; once Antipholus has abjured a logical interpretation of these weird events, they can continue to occur and he will be ready to accept them as inevitable and beyond logical inquiry and effective counter-measures. Furthermore, out of fear of worse mischief, he will even be forced to go along with some of the suggestions of these necromancers. Without this acquiescence on his part some of the subsequent events, e.g., his dining with Adriana and Luciana and his acceptance of the gold chain from Angelo would be too unmotivated to warrant audience acceptance.

Scene i, Act II re-emphasizes the identity of the Dromio who had requested the presence of Antipholus of Syracuse at dinner. The

---

[7]   Kenneth Muir, *Shakespeare's Sources*, I (London, 1957), p. 19.

audience, although it already knew as much, is reminded that the slave had invited the wrong master. The time element is again stressed, it now being mid-afternoon of our dramatic day. Adriana and Luciana are characterized by their dialogue as being of antipodal dispositions – the one jealous and shrewish, the other tolerant and gentle. Luciana delivers a homily on the rightful subjection of women to their husbands and in so doing establishes her availability and desirability as a matrimonial prospect for the unmarried Antipholus. Adriana must be shrewish enough to alienate her husband's affections but not enough to lose him; Luciana must be appealing enough to attract the attention of the foreign Antipholus so that further complications are possible and so that a love element can be added to the internal action. At the conclusion of this scene, Adriana mentions the gold chain which is later to play an important part in further ensnarling the action. A reversal of intention is seen brewing as a product of Adriana's extreme possessiveness. She would rather have her husband's love than his gift of the gold chain, but later this chain serves as a symbol of his supposedly errant love when the courtesan claims it had been promised to her. Later Adriana is in danger of having neither her husband's love nor the chain because of her unwitting exclusion of him from their home, which is motivated by this extreme possessiveness. By seeking to hang on to her husband so tenaciously she almost succeeds in losing him.

Scene ii of Act II employs another reversal of intention in Antipholus' attempt to gain an admission of pranking from his befuddled slave. Instead of achieving a solution to the mystery by gaining such an admission, he receives further conflicting testimony in Dromio's flat denial of any encounter with his master since his errand to the inn with the thousand marks.

This same scene exhibits the first in a series of repeated reversals of fortune for Dromio. From a state of happy concord with his master he is precipitously beaten and cast into disfavor. Ironic contrast is gained from the realization that slaves are rightfully beaten when they deceive or defy their masters but in these two beatings, i.e., the one administered to Dromio of Ephesus for the dinner invitation and the one administered to the other Dromio for his alleged lying, the slave is being punished for strict obedience to the commands of his master. He has performed his errand faithfully and well but he is beaten. The audience is aware of this incongruity and the humor of the situation arises from the recognition of these ridiculous reversals of fortune and the eminent likelihood of others to follow in their wake. Antipholus of Syracuse has verified the deposit of the gold at the inn and Adriana has verified the delay at the dinner table, thus informing the audience that both beatings followed upon implicit obedience on the part of the slave.

We have been prepared for Adriana's rejection by Antipholus because her slave had reported that his master had forsworn his wife. She interprets this not as a literal denial of their marriage or her identity but as an indication to her jealous nature of the transference of her husband's affections to some other woman. Thus when she confronts him, the audience is prepared to accept her forbearance of his blatant denial of her. Dromio's protest against his master's unprovoked and apparently irrational beating of him is inserted here to prepare Adriana for the courtesan's later assertion that her husband is mad.

Confusion is compounded for Antipholus of Syracuse when his slave denies having previously given him a dinner invitation. This additional confusion reinforces the notion of witchcraft in his mind, and to investigate the sorcery further he agrees to accompny Adriana and Luciana. This simple expedient actually represents a skillful solution to the difficult problem of getting the wrong husband into the house with the wife's compliance and even insistence and yet avoiding the problem of adulterous conduct. In Shakespeare's source for this section in *Amphitruo* Alcmena submits to Jupiter, who has assumed the outward form of her husband. The playwright, at this early stage of his dramatic development, is not interested in coping with a moral issue that might interfere with the comic action of the play. He further provides against skirting the problem of adulterous conduct too closely by creating the character of Luciana to serve as the legitimate object of the amorous attentions of the wandering Antipholus.

Dromio reinforces the witchcraft theme by mentioning the dire consequences to those who refuse to do the bidding of goblins and sprites. In this manner the acceptance of the dinner invitation is motivated and the exclusion of the rightful husband is anticipated.

Adriana here suffers a comic reversal of intention. She hopes to win back her supposedly errant husband's affections by getting him to come home with her, but instead she succeeds in performing an act which will definitely alienate him from her, viz., inviting a complete stranger into the privacy of her home. Luciana, conversely, experiences a fortunate reversal of intention. In attempting to reconcile her sister and brother-in-law, she succeeds in helping attract to their home an eligible young bachelor who is very strongly affected by her charm of manner and her beauty. To her it appears to be an unfortunate reversal, but to the audience it is clear that it is an auspicious one.

Here also can be seen the mingling of tones which the playwright is experimenting with. To the ludicrous tone of the basic comic plot he is adding a note of romantic love not yet fully sustained but striving toward the lyric level in Antipholus' wooing:

> O, train me not, sweet mermaid, with thy note,
> To drown me in thy sister's flood of tears.
> Sing, siren, for thyself, and I will dote;
> Spread o'er the silver waves thy golden hairs,
> And as a bed I'll take them and there lie,
> And in that glorious supposition think
> He gains by death that hath such means to die.
>
> (III, ii. 45-51)

This eloquent appeal strikes a note completely foreign to classical notions of the love of a man for a woman. Its suggestion of idealization of the love object is much at variance with the Roman carnal view of sex relations and it reflects a Renaissance attitude traceable to the influence of the love lyrics of Petrarch, Dante, and the Provençal poets.

The closing lines of Act II had been a warning to Dromio not to let anyone into the house under penalty of another beating. In view of the previous beatings, the audience is made aware that the slave will enforce these orders rigidly, thereby setting up the incongruous situation in which the husband is locked out of his own house as Mulier threatened she would do in the *Menaechmi*. In this reversal of intention Adriana wants to secure privacy with her husband and keep all others away. In attempting to achieve this, however, she succeeds only in excluding the one person she wants most to be with. The device here used of one slave denying entrance to his identical counterpart had been used in *Amphitruo* where Mercury assumes the form of the slave Sosia while Jupiter is with Alcmena and gets him to deny his own identity. Here the difference is that Shakespeare does not have the two slaves confront one another directly since such an encounter would defeat the mechanics of the plot.

Antipholus of Ephesus is accompanied by Balthazar and Angelo, the goldsmith. The presence of these companions serves two dramatic purposes. In the first place, the testimony of these two witnesses will be used later to refute Adriana's protest that she had not bolted the door against her own husband. Furthermore, through the comic disparity between the fulsome invitation tendered by the host and the rude rejection proffered by the servants, Antipholus' countermeasure is provided with a motivating circumstance. The threat of breaking down the gate, a solution that would prematurely end the laughable confusion, has to be nullified. This is the dramatic justification for Balthazar's presence in the scene. He is here to serve as an unwitting perpetrator of the confusion. It is a subtle reversal of intention that the most moderate of suggestions and the most sensible of courses of action should be precisely the thing that furthers the nonsense. Balthazar's intention is to preserve his friend's reputation as a responsible citizen by avoiding a street brawl with his wife. Actually his suggestion of their departure at this time ends the possibility of an immediate solution to the problem and sets up the loss of reputation suffered by Antipholus over the incident of the gold chain. This departure motivates the dinner at the courtesan's home and brings her into the action as a further embroiling factor. Thus we see how the playwright has skillfully used commonsense behavior set against a background of confusion to perpetuate the confusion.

The principle of action involving the repetition of reversals, besides being used with variations, must also be used with a sense of dramatic climax if it is to produce the maximum comic effect. The reversals must occur in a crescendo pattern: they must start with the relatively trivial and lead up to the significant and consequential. It is not too significant or consequential that a master administer a beating to the wrong slave. It is not too important that a slave issue a dinner invitation to the wrong master so long as the invitation is not accepted. But when two more centrally involved characters appear and repeat the invitation and thereby suffer a reversal of intention, the significance of the reversal is heightened because of its consequences and the degree of hilarity rises because of these greater consequences. These more significant consequences reach their peak in the climactic reversal of intention that occurs when one primary character takes steps against another primary character in an important action. The essence of the comic is here the same as it is in the lesser reversals – there is a disruption of the commonsense pattern of behavior – but the comic effect is heightened by the skillful order of climax proceeding from the most trivial to the most consequential reversal. There is nothing haphazard about this pattern of reversals; all is arranged so as to lead logically to one climactic reversal, which in turn leads to a resolution.

This scene contains the dramatic climax of the absurd situation. Antipholus' exclusion from his own home represents the turning-point in the action. It sends him in the direction of the courtesan who becomes one of the resolving forces in the confusion. It is she who brings Adriana out of the house and into the city, where ultimately she can be confronted with both Antipholi. All mistakes in identity subsequent to this one lead to an unwinding of the mechanism and can result only in the comic "catastrophe" of the meeting of the twins.

When mention of the chain is made as they stand outside the house, Angelo discloses that he does not have it with him. In the world of normal mishaps one might expect him to be carrying it with him since it is a gift intended for his friend and client's wife. Dramatically, however, it serves the playwright's purpose to have Angelo go in quest of it because by so doing he creates the possibility of a coincidental encounter with the other Antipholus, which encounter is necessary to further the comedy of errors. Getting the gold chain into the right hands at this stage of the action is exactly what the dramatist does not want. He needs an object to draw the courtesan into the action so that she can act as an unwitting conciliator, a clear reversal of roles for the *femme fatale*.

The romantic love theme of the Antipholus-Luciana center of action is parodied in the pursuit of Dromio by the kitchen-maid wife of his twin. The second pursuit is the comic inversion of the first. In both cases the pursued is unwilling. Luciana's resistance is motivated by a supererogatory sense of honor not by an inherent repulsion for her suitor; Dromio's attempt to escape is prompted not by any finer scruples but simply because his pursuer is coarse and ugly. Some of the comic effect of the pursuit of Dromio owes its origin to the obvious reversal of the roles in courtship, i.e., the male in this instance is the fleeing nymph, the female is the pursuing satyr. The reversal of roles in itself is comic provided the results are trivial or that any threatening serious complications are averted by mischance, coincidence, external rescue, etc. Here the underlying adultery theme is rendered trivial by the sheer ludicrousness of the situation. The kitchen maid is a mere buffoon and she is there merely to contribute to the merriment not to play any real role in the main action.

When Angelo returns with the gold chain, Antipholus of Syracuse is standing outside his brother's house with no one else on stage. Again the audience is confronted with the fact of the isolation of the comic hero and anticipates another reversal of intention. The playwright has to plan this scene so that there will be no witnesses to the transaction. Were Adriana present, she could claim the chain directly. Such a legitimate disposition of this object would thwart the subsequent *lazzi* or "stage business" it makes possible. Antipholus accepts the chain to avoid further trouble in this land of Lapland witches, but his intention is reversed for he is performing an act which will plunge him directly into trouble, with the courtesan and with Angelo again.

The necessity for creating the character of the Second Merchant, who appears in Act IV, scene i, is obvious. The playwright needs some means of initiating conflict between Angelo and Antipholus over payment for the chain. Without the pressure of time being introduced there would be less opportunity of precipitating another occasion for false identification, confusion, and comic conflict. Again the time of day is established – it is some time before five o'clock. The audience is reminded that the day is hastening to a close and that a rapid precipitation of events must occur in time for the doomed Aegeon, the central figure in the enveloping action, to be spared at sundown by a coming together of the events and characters of the enveloping action with those of the internal.

No sooner does Antipholus of Ephesus reappear on the scene than he despatches Dromio on an errand, leaving the way open again for the return of the wrong slave. This departure also serves to perpetuate the confusion by isolating him and depriving him of a witness who might refute the testimony of Angelo. The failure-to-perform-an-errand theme is repeated here on a higher level, with Angelo being upbraided for failing to fulfill his mission. A comic reversal of intention is created in Angelo's insisting on the arrest of Antipholus. He does so to make certain he will get his money, yet since this Antipholus has not actually received the goods, he is trying to get the money from the wrong man and is leaving himself vulnerable to the possibility of losing all his money and possessions through a legal suit for false arrest. The audience never considers this possibility in a serious light, however, because of its superior knowledge and anticipation that all will be set right when the dual set of twins confront one another.

With the return of Dromio of Syracuse to the stage we witness another reversal of intention. He is immediately sent on another errand, despite his protest that their ship is waiting for them in the harbor. In being sent to Adriana for the bail money he is forced to return to the place he was so anxious to escape from. By seeking out his master he had hoped to hasten his safe departure from this hag-ridden city; instead he is thrown back into the situation he preaded most.

In scene ii of this act an attempt is made to render Adriana more sympathetic and less of a conventional shrew by showing that her jealousy is motivated by love for her husband. Even in the face of strong cause for jealousy in Luciana's revelations, her actions are dominated by an acceptance of her husband's faults and an earnest

<u>desire to hold on to him</u>. Her patience and forbearance at this point, however, seem strangely inappropriate and we cannot help but feel that the playwright has manipulated character a little too clumsily in order to fit her actions into the requirements of the plot. He must have her go in search for her husband and this tolerant, solicitous attitude is needed to furnish motivation for her doing so, thus eventually bringing about the resolution and reconciliation.

In scene iii the courtesan serves as a link between Adriana and Antipholus. The liaison between her and Antipholus has been lightened from that in the *Menaechmi* to permit an easy reconciliation between the estranged man and wife. When the existence of the twin is disclosed, the courtesan will not serve as any obstacle to the reunion of husband and wife: it is only explainable error that estranges them, not infidelity or lack of affection. The courtesan is here used to add to the charge of madness against Antipholus alleged earlier by Dromio upon his return home following his beating over the dinner invitation he had given to the wrong master. In this way the playwright completes the pattern which permits the confusions to be self-perpetuating: Antipholus of Syracuse has accepted the strange events as evidences of witchcraft; the others assign the aberrant behavior to madness on the part of the Ephesian citizen. Shakespeare uses madness differently than Plautus has done. He has the diagnosis inflicted on the innocent Antipholus; whereas Plautus had Sosicles feign madness to outwit his gulls. The one's use of madness adds to the ludicrousness of the situation, the other's adds to the cynical and crass tone.

Act IV opens with another comic reversal of fortune. Dromio of Ephesus expects to be in his master's good graces for performing the rope errand, but instead he finds himself in disfavor again with a body beating administered for his pains. The Ephesian master had expected to be released from arrest on his slave's arrival with the bail money but the arrival brings a ridiculous piece of rope "out of time and out of place" and his arrest becomes definite. The arrival of Adriana is a false token of a happy reversal of fortune for Antipholus. When she sees him beating Dromio, the faithful slave who had come home for his master's bail, she is convinced that the courtesan's allegations of madness are correct. Her husband must be mad, for only a madman would punish a slave for doing what he is told. Everything Antipholus does in this encounter only succeeds in confirming her worst fears. Everything he does and says is intended to secure his freedom but instead it only assures his continued imprisonment. Beside the reversal of intention here there is also a reversal of roles. Antipholus accuses his wife of the very act he has been guilty of, namely, consorting with a paramour. The incongruity of the sallow Pinch as her paramour adds to the ridiculousness of the charge.

The confusion is deepened when Dromio confirms his master's insistence that they had been excluded from their own home but refutes his master's contention that he had sent him to Adriana for bail. In attempting to exonerate his master, Dromio's efforts are reversed and he succeeds only in giving further evidence to the charge of madness and including himself in the diagnosis. The more vigorously the pair contest the diagnosis, the more accurate it seems. In struggling violently to preserve their liberty they do the very thing which justifies the others in depriving them of liberty, and they end up bound and tied to be hauled off by the officious Pinch. The immediately ensuing arrival of the other Antipholus and Dromio with swords drawn serves to establish in the minds of Adriana, Luciana, the courtesan, and officer the correctness of the diagnosis and the dangerous aspects of the madness of the two men who have just escaped necessary and humane confinement.

In the last act the playwright's task is to immobilize one master-slave combination so that the other pair can be brought to the same spot and the true nature of the confusing situation become apparent. He accomplishes this by having Antipholus of Syracuse and Dromio seek sanctuary in the priory from what they believe to be acts of sorcery.

The homily on wifely duty delivered by the abbess to Adriana is a counterpart to Luciana's earlier remarks. It serves to reinforce her remarks on wifely submission by having them uttered by an older person wise in the ways of marital decorum and sanctified by her church connections. She serves as a univocal chorus to echo the mores of the audience's society. The abbess through skillful questioning speciously turns Adriana's own words against her so that she admits to guilt for provoking her husband to madness. She is now a subdued and tractable wife instead of a strident-voiced termagant and a happy reunion is in order now that she has been reformed. There are no other obstacles to this reunion since the liaison with the courtesan had earlier been structured as an innocuous dinner engagement.

The abbess' refusal to liberate her charges upon the demand of Adriana is a device to bring the Duke into the internal action. His is the only authority that can supersede that of the abbess. Up until now his role has been that of a stage-setter and prompter in the expository part of the enveloping action. The merchant's mention of the hour being five brings back the time of Aegeon's execution and correlates the two plots temporally. The solution to both the internal and enveloping action must now be effected. With the Duke's arrival we are reminded that payment of the sum of one thousand marks will save the condemned man's life. The audience will soon be rewarded for its indulgence in anticipating the saving of the father's life by his own sons.

The arrival of the messenger with the news that Antipholus and Dromio have escaped their bonds is the harbinger of the solution. Adriana already "knows" they have escaped by virtue of her own senses and sanity about which there is no question. This new confusing bit of news cannot be attributed to her husband's "madness" and calls for a flat rejection of its truth or for further investigation along commonsense lines that will produce the right answer. With one set of twins immobilized in the priory, the appearance of the other set on the scene brings an end to the playwright's adroit manipulations. The presence of both sets in the same place at the same time is the thing that he scrupulously avoided for four previous acts; now he just as sedulously pursues its realization. The comedy of errors has depended on the concatenation of coincidences which permitted master to encounter slave but never permitted master to encounter master or slave to encounter slave. With the Duke on the scene, the playwright is equipped with a resolving agent. The Duke need do nothing more than command that the abbess bring forth her charges.

Before the happy denouement, however, the comedy comes near

pathos in Aegeon's fruitless appeal for aid to Antipholus of Ephesus. This is the one confusion of identities in the play that is not comic. Instead of being made the butt of the comedy the old man is made a pathetic figure. The pathos is produced by Aegeon's acceptance of his son's denial as an understandable result of the changes that care and time have wrought in his visage. Since he does not protest, there is no comic conflict. The tension and tone are no longer comic and the playwright relieves it immediately. At this brush with pathos, the abbess appears with Antiphlous of Syracuse and Dromio and all is instantly clear. With the resolution of the internal action with its series of mistaken identities, the enveloping action is also resolved. Aegeon is reunited with Aemilia, who had become an abbess after the loss of her set of twins to kidnappers. The death sentence, the long separation, the estrangement between husband and wife, the misappropriated chain, the courtesan's ring, the rope, the ducats are all forgotten in the general merriment and felicitations following upon the mutual recognitions and ducal amnesty.

With this happy, sentimental outcome we can see that the playwright has turned the material of Plautine farce to a new use. In Plautus the *cognitio* had no significance beyond offering a resolution to the comic entanglement. In Shakespeare the *cognitio*, set as it is against a pathetic-romantic background, serves not only to bring clarity into the comic confusion but also to bring happiness into the somber situation. A whole series of reversals of intention on the comic level is contained within the framework of one serious reversal of fortune – the change from a death penalty to a last minute reprieve and happy family reunion. We can see that the playwright has added the tone of pathos to the ludicrous one of farce. It is an elementary harmony that he achieves here but this tentative mixture of antithetical tones represents a successful experiment. Comic and pathetic tones can be combined in one play to the enhancement of both. Shakespeare has learned that he does not have to be content with a pure specimen of either the comic or the serious.

The Roman farce did not contain the serious, let alone the pathetic. All pathetic possibilities had been eliminated by relegating them to the prologue or by submerging them in stereotyped characters. Besides using a serious reversal of fortune in the enveloping action to introduce the element of the pathetic, Shakespeare also brings in the element of the strange and marvelous adventure beset with perils which is the essence of romance and contrasts sharply with the mundane realism of farce.

The attempt to correlate the comic reversals with character is a further step away from Plautine farce in which the reversals are almost exclusively the result of coincidence. Shakespeare attempts to differentiate the characters of the two masters, the two slaves, the women, and even of some of the lesser characters so that the reversals will seem to emanate from character instead of from mere coincidence. Antipholus of Ephesus is depicted as being hot-tempered and sulky so that his precipitous decision to dine with the courtesan will seem plausible. Antipholus of Syracuse is shown as being good-humored, impressionable, and sentimental so that his initial acceptance of the confusion is made likely and so that his courtship of Luciana is made acceptable to her and to the audience. The pranking nature and cleverness of Dromio of Syracuse are used as a motive force in the plot as is the obtuseness and clownishness of the Ephesian slave.

The most significant attempt to relate the reversals with character is made in the depiction of Adriana. From the totally unattractive Mulier of Plautus she is changed into a jealous, possessive woman genuinely in love with her husband, capable of reformation, and worthy of reconciliation. Luciana's reversal of fortune, i.e., from virginity to marriage is brought about by feminity, honesty, and loyalty. She confides all to her sister, and this frankness ironically leads to a happy resolution in which she finds a husband.

In this early effort Shakespeare is primarily concerned with the mechanics of plot, especially with the manipulation and multiplication of ironic reversals. As his main agencies of plot movement, he uses a motivating circumstance outside the main action – the shipwreck – and multiple accident and coincidence within the main plot, centering about two sets of identical twins whose destinies are intertwined. The central farcical tone is contrasted with a tone of pathos by wrapping the main incidents in an enveloping action involving the impending execution of Aegeon, the destitute old father of the twins in search for his long-lost wife and sons. This pathetic counter-tone lends significance to the denouement beyond that of simple comic *anagnorisis*. In this attempt to master the structuring and climactic arrangement of ironic reversals and to balance contrasting tones, beauty of language is neglected except for a few felicitous touches. Although characterization is elementary, he does experiment with the creation of the romantic heroine. His success here is very limited, but the attempt indicates that he is experimenting with character as a force to initiate and sustain the desired comic or serious action.

II. *LOVE'S LABOUR'S LOST*

From a comedy of situation operating on the level of farce with laughter resulting from ironic reversals brought about by coincidence and improbability, we turn to a comedy of artificial conventions with laughter resulting from the conflict between affectation and natural humor. The affectations treated include pseudo-celibacy, gongorism, and pedantry, their natural antagonists being love between the sexes, the poetic and witty use of language, and rustic common sense. The structure of the play centers about the creation of characters which embody these affectations and their opposites and the arrangement of incidents which bring them into conflict and lead to a resolution in which nature triumphs over affectation.

As in *The Comedy of Errors* the playwright uses a serious enveloping action which contrasts with the tone of the main action and brings about the resolution of the central conflict – that between celibacy and love. Unlike that play, however, this comedy uses a separately developed C plot involving a conflict between the affectation of gongorism and its antithesis, true wit. This C plot takes the form of a love triangle exposing the hypocrisy of the gongorist and parodying the love story in the main action or B plot.

With the emphasis on affectation and its display, the dramatist's attention is centered on language and atmosphere. The arrangement and complication of incident is placed second to wit and poetry, one retarding the action, the other contributing little to its forward movement.

In attempting a structural analysis of Shakespeare's early comedies one is forced to consider the question of relative, if not exact, dates of composition because of the light such knowledge may shed on the playwright's progress from apprenticeship to mastery in his craft. Unfortunately scholarship has not unequivocally established precise dates of composition or even the exact sequence of plays in Shakespeare's early years as a dramatist. One is forced to conjecture on the basis of limited external and treacherous internal evidence. Eminent scholars will differ widely on the dating of any particular play. At times they may be as many as six years apart in their dates, and their arrangements of the plays chronologically may be at distressingly wide variance with one another.

The problem of dating *Love's Labour's Lost* is just such a case. There are certain facts which are undisputed, yet there is far from any unanimity in assigning the play to any particular year. Estimates range from the somewhat astounding one of 1578, which denies authorship to Shakespeare in favor of de Vere,[1] to the more orthodox conjecture of 1595.[2] There are others, however, who argue that it should be dated somewhere between August of 1588 and August of 1589.[3] If the last estimate is the correct one, it would mean that *Love's Labour's Lost* is the earliest of Shakespeare's extant comedies.

One of the undisputed facts concerning the dating is that a quarto edition of the play was published in 1598 with the title page carrying the following announcement: "A Pleasant Conceited Comedie Called, Loues Labors lost. As it was presented before her Highness this last Christmas. Newly corrected and augmented by W. Shakespere. Imprinted at London W. W. for Cutbert Burby. 1598." This edition may have been set into type from the original manuscript, a manuscript which was apparently confusing, at least to a novice printer, who produced a badly botched printed copy. This printed copy shows definite evidence that in several places, particularly in Acts IV and V, key speeches have been re-written and augmented.

---

[1] Eva Turner Clark, *The Satirical Comedy "Love's Labor's Lost"* (New York, 1933), p. 10.
[2] Edmund K. Chambers, *William Shakespeare* (London, 1924), I, p. 333.
[3] T. W. Baldwin, *William Shakespere's Five-Act Structure* (Urbana, 1947), p. 579.

A copy of this Quarto containing some revisions was no doubt the basis of the text of the play as it appears in the First Folio. The words "newly corrected and augmented" appearing on the title page of the Quarto suggest that an earlier edition of the play might have appeared in print unauthorized by the playwright or his company. Pollard believes that this Quarto was very likely preceded by such a pirated earlier edition, of which no trace remains except in the elusive phrase "newly corrected and augmented". Since no copy of such a hypothetical earlier edition, pirated or authorized, has survived, we can only reason by analogy with the printing history of *Romeo and Juliet* that such an earlier printing did exist. A first quarto of the latter play exists which is considerably different from the second, inferior to it, and probably pirated.[4]

The only importance of these editions, actual and supposed, is the degree of "correction" and "augmentation" they represent. Did the playwright take an older play just prior to Christmas 1597–98 and revise it extensively, with considerable structural re-working, or did he merely polish and expand a speech here and there to make a point more clearly? The results of the structural analysis attempted here would support the view that the revisions were relatively minor and that the play remains substantially what it was when it was first written. If Shakespeare had been making extensive structural revisions in a comedy as late as 1598, one would expect that he would exploit what he had learned about the construction of a multi-level, tonally contrasting plot to its maximum use. It is true he uses a tonally contrasting C plot, but it is not fully developed. Furthermore, he is awkward in his use of Holofernes and Nathaniel, who appear to belong to the C plot and yet are really not a part of it. By 1598, if he were revising a play extensively, he very likely would have constructed a D plot that had an intricately worked out relationship with both the C and the B plots. Here he uses the potential elements of a D plot in the persons of Holofernes and Nathaniel in the periphery of the C plot and in a masque sequence loosely related to the B plot. Such an

[4] A. W. Pollard, *Shakespeare's Fight with the Pirates* (Cambridge, 1920), p. 103.

imperfect use of the elements of the A-B-C-D plot structure would perhaps suggest that at the time of writing this play Shakespeare had not arrived at the formula he perfected in *A Midsummer Night's Dream*.

Quiller-Couch and Wilson argue for a special private performance as the occasion for the initial presentation of the play,

We give it as our belief and no more, that *Love's Labour's Lost* was written in 1593 for a private performance in the house of some grandee who had opposed Raleigh and Raleigh's "men" – possibly the Earl of Southampton's.[5]

In this same year Shakespeare's *Venus and Adonis* had been dedicated to the young Earl of Southampton. The young nobleman had refused to marry despite the urging of his guardian, Lord Burleigh, and it is therefore not improbable that love, or rather a disdain for love, was the theme which occupied the witty young men of Southampton's household. The theme of young men who despised love was thus ready at hand for the playwright to fashion a lightly satirical bit of entertainment.

The only trouble with this conjecture is that it would seem to place Shakespeare on the wrong side of the controversy. The theme of the play is clearly intended to reprimand gently such young men as Southampton for following false lights. If this were written to entertain the Earl of Southampton and his friends, it would be rather risky entertainment to provide one's patron with. It would seem more likely that the play was designed to appeal to a feminine audience, or one dominated by a strong feminine bias, by elevating women to a position of pre-eminence over any weightier activities a courtier might engage in, such as difficult abstract studies like science and mathematics. Rather than assigning the initial performance to the Earl's hall, one might more reasonably assign it to the court with the Queen being entertained by the flattering notion that a courtier's duty is to spend his time in the study of ways to please a clever and demanding woman.

[5] Sir Arthur Quiller-Couch and John Dover Wilson, *Love's Labour's Lost* (Cambridge, 1923), p. xii.

Although the problems of dating and the nature of the audience for which the play was written may provide some information on Shakespeare's development as a dramatist and on the tone of this particular play, the problem of interpreting obscure topical allusions and identifying supposed prototypes for the various characters will be ignored here as being irrelevant to matters of structure. The meaning of "the school of night" and "the charge school" on the hill will be left for others to fathom.[6]

Just as the problems of dating, first performance, and topicality are frustratingly elusive, so is the tracking down of sources and analogues relatively unrewarding. All that one learns of value here is that there is a pseudo-historical background for the play and that the names of the chief characters have been borrowed from contemporary French history. The central idea that a prince with scholarly pretensions binds himself and his close associates to an artificial monastic way of life which is shattered by the intrusion of women would seem too commonplace to have been the original invention of Shakespeare; yet no earlier work, either of fiction or of history, has been discovered which can reasonably be regarded as a source for the play.[7]

Apparently, then, Shakespeare was here trying to invent a plot of his own; in *The Comedy of Errors* he had relied on the structure of Plautine comedy, a very substantial prop for a novice playwright. All he had to do there was to revamp an already well constructed play. He did this primarily by converting the expository material into a tonally contrasting enveloping action or A plot and by increasing the possibilities of mistaken identities through the creation of a second set of twins. Otherwise, aside from abortive attempts at characterization, he follows the Plautine pattern of arranging meetings under real identities, then under false identities, and back again under real identities. In *Love's Labour's Lost* he has much more to do: he has to construct his own original situation, his own complications leading to a climax, and his own resolution.

---

[6] Frances A. Yates, *A Study of "Love's Labour's Lost"* (Cambridge, 1936), pp. 20-26.

[7] *Love's Labour's Lost*, ed. Wilbur Cross and Tucker Brooke (New Haven, 1925), p. 127.

That he does not succeed as well here in his B plot is not surprising considering his relative inexperience and the lack of an exact model to follow. Given a theme, a cast of pseudo-historical personages, and a basic blocking situation he tries to construct a series of incidents depending for their comic effect not on confusions of identity but on conflicts between affectation and nature in high and low society. It is the development of the lesser elements of the conflict on the level of low society that offers a feature that had not existed in the Plautine structure and which overshadows his relative failure in the main plot.

Like the main action of the play, these lesser elements appear also to owe little to Shakespeare's reading. They may have been suggested to him by other theatrical performances which he saw. Several characters in the play are closely akin to conventionalized types in the Italian Commedia dell'Arte: Armado is clearly the grandiloquent braggart who owes his ultimate origin to the *miles gloriosus* of classical comedy; Moth is the zany who is always paired with the braggart in Italian improvised comedy; Holofernes is the pedant; Nathaniel, the parasite; Costard, the slow-witted rustic, here transformed; and Dull, the stupid magistrate. Some of these characters are identified by the conventional names in parts of the text.

Whatever the degree of debt to Italian improvised comedy in the way of adaptation of stock comic figures, there is no doubt of Shakespeare's debt to John Lyly. Heavy as it is, this indebtedness is not that of a slavish imitator but of one who is striving after a new form of comedy with the artifice of Lyly as the starting point. There is a decided structural resemblance between *Love's Labour's Lost* and two of Lyly's plays, *Endimion* and *Gallathea*.

This resemblance of the fantastical Spaniard and his page to Lyly's knight and page is so close that one can scarcely doubt that Shakes-

The chief points of connexion between *Endimion* and *Love's Labour's Lost* would be the four couples in each, and on the comic side the magnificent Armado chaffed by his page Moth and declining on Jaquenetta, as Sir Thopas is chaffed by Epiton and subsides on Bagoa.[8]

8 R. W. Bond, *The Complete Works of John Lyly* (Oxford, 1902), II, p. 276.

peare is here borrowing from his highly successful predecessor in English comedy. Only Holofernes and his crew are extraneous to the structure of *Endimion* and they may not have been in the original play but may have been added later as part of the "newly corrected and augmented" material promised in the Quarto edition of 1598.

Shakespeare's debt to Lyly does not stop with the borrowing of symmetrical character groupings and chief supporting characters. It is further evidenced in a crucial mechanical detail that propels the action forward toward the comic catastrophe. This time the borrowing is not from *Endimion* but from *Gallathea.*

The scene in *Gallathea* (ii.i.) where Diana's nymphs, entering one by one, confess their broken vow and agree to pursue their passion, has often been quoted as the original of that between the four anchorites, which is dramatically the best in *Love's Labour's Lost*[9]

This scene is the core of the action of the play. It represents the climax of the action and furnishes the motive force for the third and fourth acts.

The evidence above, then, would suggest that not only the symmetrical characters but also the general structure of *Love's Labour's Lost* can be traced to Lyly. This structural borrowing extends down into the subplot parody on the main romantic plot, but with a definite breaking away from its restrictions. As Lyly had used Sir Thopas and Epiton's wit combats as a parody of the main plot, so does Shakespeare use Armado and Moth for the same purpose. The difference arises, however, in the creation of Costard by the younger dramatist to act as a rival to Armado, thereby creating a full parody of the romantic main plot in the Spaniard's pompous courtship of the wench Jaquenetta. The apprentice dramatist has improved on the use of the parodying subplot, but he has learned the principle of it from his older contemporary.

In addition to the structural details and character groupings Shakespeare may also have borrowed and adapted Lyly's theme. In *Endimion* the theme centers about the conflict between love and friendship; in *Love's Labour's Lost* it centers about the polar natures of love and learning. Although the themes are not identical,

[9] Bond, II, p. 297.

they are obviously related in their polarization of a *modus vivendi.*
So also is the delicate fashioning of Lylean diction easily traceable
in the language of *Love's Labour's Lost.* A king and three lords
engage in with combats with a Princess and three ladies with a
brilliant display of verbal subtleties cleverly bandied about from
one pair of lovers to another. In the climactic discovery scene there
is a progression of poetry and wit from one young lord to the next
and then back again. In the Russian masque scene each young man
in turn and his feminine adversary entertain the audience with their
verbal bouts. There is an artificial brilliance about the whole thing.
The young dramatist seems engaged in a verbal juggling act that
he is not quite satisfied with as evidenced by his importation of
Holofernes and Nathaniel with a consequent unbalancing of the
fragile Lylean structure. He seems to be aware that all this delicate
symmetry and balance are dominating the structure of the play
rather than contributing to it, and he appears to be searching for a
way out of the restrictive formula.

In later plays this search for a way out leads Shakespeare quite
a distance from the artifice of Lyly, but in this play at least he does
owe a clear debt to this fashioner of stylized comedy. In light of this
clear debt to Lyly it would seem that any pursuit of a source related
to the historical content of the play would be pointless. Rather
than attempting a political or historical play, Shakespeare was
probably simply taking advantage of a current interest in France
and French personages of importance to fashion a court play after
the model of the master of court plays, John Lyly. "Navarre",
"Berowne", "Dumain", "Longaville", "Boyet", etc. are names
that the playwright chose to give his characters in order to lend an
elegant tone to his dramatically stylized treatment of the love-
versus-learning theme, a theme which was part of the intellectual
climate of his day, at least among the leisured nobility for whom
this play seems clearly intended.

The elegant stylization of the play can easily be seen in a cursory
examination of the plot. As a protest against the usual preoccupation of courtiers, the King of Navarre resolves to make his court
"a little Academe" with the aid of his three noble friends, Berowne,
Longaville, and Dumain. Berowne argues against the practicality

of the plan and predicts that they will all be forsworn many times over before the stipulated three-year period is out, but his objections fall on deaf ears. Reluctantly, he agrees to bind himself with the others to fasting, sleeping only three hours a night, and completely eschewing the company of women. The only diversion they will permit themselves from their arduous philosophical pursuits will be the conversation of Don Armado, "one who the music of his own vain tongue doth ravish like enchanting harmony". No sooner is their compact subscribed to, however, before it is threatened by a breach from without. In his scholarly enthusiasm, the King has forgotten completely about the diplomatic mission of the Princess of France to his court for the purpose of settling an old debt existing between him and her father, the King of France. To complicate matters the Princess is accompanied on her mission by three charming and vivacious ladies. Despite his solemn vow, the King is constrained to unbend and extend them some measure of hospitality.

Before the arrival of this entourage, the first transgression of the compact is reported by Constable Dull in the form of a letter from Don Armado, who has apprehended Costard, a rustic, with Jaquenetta, a country wench, with whom Don Armado himself is so smitten that he has fallen into a profound melancholy in which his thoughts are all directed toward sonneteering his loved one. As punishment for his flagrant transgression, Costard is placed in Armado's custody for a week of fasting on bran and water.

Since the impractical compact which he has devised renders it impossible for him to extend the full hospitality of his court to his diplomatic visitors, King Ferdinand has to resort to a compromise whereby he attempts to make the ladies as comfortable as possible in a pavilion in the park outside his palace. During the ensuing conduct of the diplomatic mission the King falls in love with the Princess, and each of the three lords falls in love with one of the ladies.

At the same time the enraptured Armado, in order to convey the depths of his grand passion, releases Costard from imprisonment to serve as his letter carrier to Jaquenetta. On his way to deliver the letter, Costard is met by Berowne, who also entrusts him with a love letter, this one addressed to Rosaline, the dark beauty among the companions of the Princess.

The letters get mixed in transit: Costard delivers Armado's wordy rhetoric to Rosaline, who, along with the other ladies, is much amused by it. Berowne's poetic avowal of love is delivered to Jaquenetta. Unable to read, she gives the letter to Holofernes, the village schoolmaster, so that he may inform her of its contents. He realizes that the verses are the work of one of the alleged votaries to learning, and he sends them to the King by way of Jaquenetta and Costard.

Berowne, meanwhile, bemoaning his lover's state, conceals himself when he sees the King approaching and overhears him reciting a poem in praise of his mistress, the Princess. At the approach of Longaville, the King hides and both he and Berowne eavesdrop on this lord's love-struck poetizing of Maria. The process is repeated with the arrival of Dumain with his sonnet in praise of Katherine. Longaville reveals his presence to reprove Dumaine, the King reproves Longaville, and Berowne appears to chide all three derelict companions for their forswearing themselves. At this moment Costard and Jaquenetta appear with written proof of Berowne's similar dereliction. Realizing that their compact was a foolish one, they all agree that women are the books, the arts, the academes that nourish all the world. To woo and win their ladies they plan revels, masques, and dances, but they suffer some misgivings that they may be punished for being forsworn.

After having dispatched presents to their mistresses, the lords disguise themselves as Muscovites in preparation for their visit to the pavilion of the Princess and her fair companions. The clever young ladies are informed of their coming by Boyet, the Princess' advisor, and they exchange favors so that each of the young men will be wooing the wrong lady. This ruse confounds the lovers and their Muscovite masquerade ends in fiasco. They return to their ladies in their own guise and are compelled to listen to the ladies' disdainful tale of the ridiculous "mess of Russians" who visited them. The men are forced to confess their subterfuge and acknowledge the cleverness of the ladies.

In the meantime, the village schoolmaster and the curate, along

with Armado, Moth, and Costard, have also prepared an entertainment. Their presentation of a pageant of the Nine Worthies before
the sophisticated ladies and lords is productive of much unconscious
humor.

Into the midst of this scene of merriment a messenger arrives with
the news that the King of France is dead. The Princess is thus
compelled by duty to return home without delay. Ferdinand
proposes openly for the hands of the ladies for himself and his
courtiers, but in punishment for their foolish oath and for forswearing themselves, the ladies assign them penances adapted to their
personal shortcomings and postpone their answers for a year and a
day.

A backward glance at the plot shows the appropriateness of
Northrup Frye's observation that "the movement of comedy is
usually a movement from one kind of society to another".
The play opens with the obstructing or humorous characters in
control of events, in this case the King of Navarre and his pseudo-
anchorites. The audience is soon made aware that they are usurpers,
i.e., antagonists of "common sense". Toward the end of the
play the resolution is brought about by a comic discovery which
destroys the integrity of the usurping society and permits its antithesis, the rightful society, to be established with the concurrence
and delight of the audience.

This movement of comedy from one society to another has been
compared to that in a lawsuit in which the contending parties hold
different versions of the same situation. The plaintiffs in the suit,
here the Princess and her entourage, prove that their version of the
facts is the real one and that the view held by the defendant King
and his lords is an illusory one that deserves to be abandoned.
The *Tractatus Coislinianus*, a short work closely related to Aristotle's
Poetics, divides the *dianoia* of comedy into two parts: "opinion",
representing the false society; and "proof", representing the true or
desirable society. These proofs take the form of oaths, compacts,
witnesses, ordeals, and laws.

In *Love's Labour's Lost* the celibacy and study compact and the
oaths taken upon it form the basis of the false or unrealistic society.
The arrival of the diplomatic mission staffed by beautiful young

ladies constitutes the trial by ordeal which establishes the essential
"illegality" of any compact which attempts to create a society
excluding women and love. The King has misused his rights by
attempting to create such an unrealistic, humorous society, and the
pseudo-utopia he has whimsically hoped to create is destroyed by
its first encounter with reality or truth. This society of ritual bond-
age is akin symbolically to death and has to be routed by the forces
of youth and life. The triumphant society represents the forces of
life untrammeled by restrictive oaths at variance with "nature"
and "commonsense".

With the opening speech of King Ferdinand we are acquainted
with the artificial restrictions which he is attempting to impose on
the forces of life.

> Therefore, brave conquerors – for so you are
> That war against your own affections
> And the huge army of the world's desires –
> Our late edict shall strongly stand in force.
> Navarre shall be the wonder of the world;
> Our court shall be a little Academe,
> Still and contemplative in living art.
> You three, Berowne, Dumain, and Longaville,
> Have sworn for three years' term to live with me
> My fellow scholars, and to keep those statutes
> That are recorded in this schedule here.
> Your oaths are passed, and now subscribe your names,
> That his own hand may strike his honor down
> That violates the smallest branch herein.
> If you are armed to do as sworn to do,
> Subscribe to your deep oaths, and keep it too. (I.i. 11-23)

The audience is made aware from the start that this attempt to
create an artificial society is doomed to failure, that this war
against the "affections" and "huge army of the world's desires"
will end in comic disaster. The oath sworn to is the constitution of
the new society, but it is a society at war with itself because it
depends on the human affections, bravery and honor, to war against
other human affections, love and desire, in defense of an absurd
compact. The subscribers to this oath are doomed to disaster, but
since this is a comedy, the disaster will take the form of their

conversion to "normality" and participation in the "natural" society defended by the proponents of human emotion, the Princess and her *escadron volante*. These comic "usurpers" will not be destroyed as punishment for their deviation from the normal. Instead they will be punished by ridicule, but they will be allowed, after suitable penance, to return to the society of those representing normalcy.

What determines the comic in drama is the standard of "common sense" against which the alleged deviation is juxtaposed. The nature of the audience's customs and beliefs determines what the norm is that the play will hold up as the desirable society which the comic or humorous figures are attempting to depose. In this instance, the undesirable society is depicted as one in which celibacy, study, and fasting reign – a pseudo-monastic existence. The desirable society, by converse, is depicted as one in which love, wit, and festivity reign. Berowne serving as the *eiron*, or ironic critic, attacks the tenets of the King as *alazon*, or proponent of the comic order,

> Why, all delights are vain, but that most vain
> Which, with pain purchased, doth inherit pain–
> As painfully to pore upon a book
> To seek the light of truth, while truth the while
> Doth falsely blind the eyesight of his look.
> Light, seeking light, doth light of light beguile;
> So, ere you find where light in darkness lies,
> Your light grows dark by losing of your eyes.
> Study me how to please the eye indeed,
> By fixing it upon a fairer eye,
> Who dazzling so, that eye shall be his heed,
> And give him light that it was blinded by. (I.i. 72-83)

Here the desirable society is depicted as one in which the beauty and intelligence of women as mirrored in their eyes is the proper study and occupation for mankind. This would suggest that the play was written with the purpose of vindicating women and love from the attacks of a group of detractors who would relegate them to a position of inferiority or eliminate them entirely from the life of the young noble. It is worthwhile remembering here that our first extant edition of the play, the Quarto of 1598, mentions that the play had been performed before the Queen. This is exactly the type of entertainment that would be calculated to please a demanding queen anxious to keep her brilliant young courtiers from becoming too seriously devoted to anything but her and her court activities. The nature of the King's edict would support the theory that the original audience for which the play was written was very likely not that of the ordinary public theatres but of some select private hall. The central theme supposes a set of biases which are distinctly those of the court and the nobility, especially of the feminine portion, and has little in it to suit the bias of the average Londoner. The general theme – nature versus affectation – would appeal to a miscellaneous audience, but the working out of the theme in the play is too specifically courtly to permit the general theme, nature-versus-affectation, to override the specific one, the proper study of young men is the beauty and spirit of young ladies not the knotty, abstruse problems of philosophy. Some of the shortcomings of the play as a comedy arise from the narrowness of the central theme; it was designed to appeal to too select an audience. Great comedy appeals to the generality of men in any society; a lesser form of comedy is satisfied to appeal to the biases of a select group. Within the limits of what he was attempting to do here, however, the playwright's efforts can be considered as being reasonably successful. His select audience is provided with a series of related situations in which the proponents of its cherished beliefs triumph over those who would destroy its system of values by establishing a society based on antithetical principles. This triumph of courtly dalliance over study was no doubt highly gratifying to his select audience, but since not enough of us share its biases, the play has a limited appeal in its central comic reversal and comes to life only in its subsidiary characters and scenes or in its poetry and spectacle rather than in its basic conflict.

On the larger scale, the playwright is attempting to use humor as the vindicator of the natural as opposed to the affected. This is a situational device that could easily be productive of genuine humor, but the execution here falls somewhat short of the conception. The lack of genuine humor, humor being defined as the product of a marked disparity between what is and what should be, arises from the playwright's selecting as his norm or natural something equally as close to affectation as is the supposed deviation. Humor is supposed to arise from the head-on conflict between affectation and what purports to be nature. It can be stated almost axiomatically that where the concept of nature is a narrow one, one confined to the tastes and prejudices of a highly specialized audience, in this case an Elizabethan courtly one, the humor runs the serious risk of lacking broad appeal and deteriorating into conventional highly stylized games catering to the whims of a group unrepresentative of the sense of comic disparity of most of us. This is precisely what happened to Lylean comedy with its symmetrically paired lovers and their courtly word-play. It needed the silken atmosphere of court and could not survive in the russet environment of the public playhouse, the true arbiter of the universally comic. In this play it is only where the humor breaks the confines of the courtly via the presence of Costard, Dull, Holofernes, and Nathaniel that it gains universality and provokes real mirth rather than a sophisticated, knowing smile at a wit-bout well played. When the gap between the affectation and normalcy is great, laughter results; when the standard of normalcy is as much at variance with ordinary "commonsense", no real laughter results except, perhaps, in a way unintended by the playwright.

Considerable pleasure, it is true, may be derived from other aspects of the play – from the poetry, music, or spectacle, but the central situation in itself and in the manner it is worked out is not a sufficiently comic one. Too often the play relies on diction and spectacle for its appeal instead of on the basic dramatic elements of character and action.

The comic action in the play centers about the exposure of the unnaturalness of the social regimen which the King and his companions have naively and rashly pledged themselves to.

> That is, to live and study here three years.
> But there are other strict observances –
> As not to see a woman in that term,
>
> . . . .
>
> And one day in a week to touch no food,
> And but one meal on every day beside,

. . . .
And then to sleep but three hours in the night,
And not be seen to wink of all the day—   (I.i. 35-43)

The King and his fellow celibates are made young, two of them even callow, to render the basic incongruity most striking. Old men might be expected to resist, and perhaps successfully, the pleasures and demands of the flesh, but young men, never. The notion of study in itself is not reprehensible or unnatural, but it is contaminated and condemned by the unnaturally austere company it is forced to keep. The same pact enjoining them to study also demands that they resist the normal requirements of human life: food and sleep. Not only will they fast one day a week, which is a rigorous enough prescription in itself, but they must so punish their weary bodies so as not even to permit their tired lids to droop in a momentary wink. Such demands for perfection far beyond the scope of youth and nature are ridiculous on the face of them and are doomed to failure no matter how vigorous the protestations in their behalf.

Any society built on such absurd protocols cannot survive, and Berowne is given the role of *eiron* to attack the practicability of the prescribed rituals. Since the new society is one at variance with common sense and nature, the *eiron* serves as a vocal medium for the inarticulate protests of the audience. The *eiron* is stilled in his protests by the rigid insistence of the *alazon* and his supporters, but we know that his view, which is that of the audience, will prevail in the end and the usurpers will be routed. His cry of protest:

> Oh, these are barren tasks, too hard to keep;
> Not to see ladies, study, fast, not sleep!

expresses exactly the sentiments of the audience, and the ensuing action of the play will be concerned with vindicating this protest.

The playwright has structured his situation so that a major reversal of intention is imminent in it. In their attempt to escape women and the other appeals to the senses, the votaries create a situation in which they will be rendered most vulnerable. Their absurd oath, blatantly proclaimed, will serve as a challenge for those opposed to its terms, and the extreme restrictions they place on themselves and others will only operate to enhance the irresistibility of the temptations they have vowed to avoid.

The audience is not left to conjecture how this downfall will occur. It is immediately supplied with an object lesson of the power of nature to destroy artificial restraint. With the entrance of Dull and Costard we have the natural world impinging on the artificial. A reversal of roles is created in the incorporating of the *homme moyen sensuel* into the society of those governed by the restrictive covenants. He is charged, tried, and found guilty by laws that he had no part in making and no desire to subscribe to. He represents the norm on a lower social scale, in fact, on an almost animalistic one. This is the unsophisticated, natural man ruled by his desires and appetites, comically bewildered at the thought that such innocent activity warrants condemnation and punishment. There is a complete absence of hypocrisy; in his innocence Costard sees nothing to be denied or repudiated. It is inconceivable to him that anyone would wish to curb natural desire and prevent its fulfilment. Fasting is all right so long as one has a full belly.

This artificial life agreed to by compact produces the ludicrous situation in which a man is punished for something which he instinctively knows is not wrong. He has offended against no one, and no one involved in his act has lodged a charge against him. Where artificiality engenders an uncomprehending protest of innocence on Costard's part, it fosters lip-service and hypocritical conformity amongst presumed supporters of the celibacy pact. In Armado, "the refined traveler of Spain", we have the self-deceived, zealous hypocrite who would punish in Costard the very thing he himself is guilty of. Here again the playwright is using the device of reversal of roles: one of those designated to preserve the absurd law is the one most consumed with desire to violate it. Since Costard had never agreed to the compact, it cannot be said that he committed any real violation. His plight is comical because he is punished, i.e., suffers a reversal of fortune for something he did not do as Dromio is punished for disobedience he was not guilty of. Armado, on the other hand, has subscribed to the edict. His actions become comical because of the incongruity between what he ostensibly subscribes to and what he actually does. He suffers a reversal of intention and of fortune in that by attempting to enforce the law he leads himself into the violation of it. The tone here becomes satirical insofar as the basis of the comic is the recognition of hypocrisy.

Structurally a polarization is set up between the affected Spaniard and the unpretentious rustic. The former represents false wit and hypocrisy; the latter, natural wit and unabashed candor. We are warned in advance about Armado in the conversation between the King and his associates:

> ... Our Court, you know, is haunted
> With a refinéd traveler of Spain –
> A man in all the world's new fashion planted
> That hath a mint of phrases in his brain;
> One whom the music of his own vain tongue
> Doth ravish like enchanting harmony;   (I.i. 163-168)

Since his affected speech is the most striking feature about him, we are given a sample of this before we get to see him in person. When Dull brings in the accused Costard, he has with him a letter from Armado specifying the charges. The contest between the unaffected wit of Costard and the false wit of the Spaniard is seen in the speech of the swain. The letter starts with a florid salutation, "Great Deputy, the welkin's vice-regent, and sole dominator of Navarre, my soul's earth's god and body's fostering patron". Costard immediately protests, "Not a word of Costard yet". The letter continues in its exaggerated Gongoristic vein and, after many circumlocutions and extravagances of style, finally states the charge against Costard, namely, that of consorting with the obliging Jaquenetta. The simplicity of the alleged crime is out of all proportion to the ostentatious wording of the accusation. The humor is compounded by Costard's wittily resorting to a parody of the fantastical Spaniard's language in his quibble over "wench", "damsel", "virgin", "maid", etc. whereby the rustic seeks to evade technical guilt by resorting to tricks of language: the act was not reprehensible in itself; it is only some subtlety of language that now renders it so. Therefore, he, Costard, will engage in few subtleties of language of his own and thereby escape punishment. In this first engagement in the lists, then, nature triumphs over affectation in the production of humor, although affectation has won a temporary victory by subduing and restraining nature for the occasion.

But the audience knows that this rigid state of affairs cannot long endure and that the ebullient spirits of nature and the liberating influence of common sense exemplified on a gross level by Costard will triumph over the sterile affectation and ritualistic behavior of Armado. The compact of the King and his courtiers has to be viewed against this elemental conflict. Clearly the King and his fellow celibates are on the side of affectation and folly, and they too will encounter their Costards and Jaquenettas. Life will break in upon them, triumphing over sterility and ritual, the perpetual antagonists of the comic spirit.

Life, for Ferdinand and his fellow academicians, takes the form of the Princess of France and her ladies-in-waiting. They are Jaquenettas in silks instead of jersey, but Jaquenettas they are nonetheless, as their bawdy word-play with Boyet attests. The news that they are coming immediately introduces the comic nemesis into the main action and suggests the necessary comic catastrophe, or major reversal, that must result. The compact stipulates behavior so obviously artificial and contrary to common sense that it must disintegrate in the face of all the social and natural pressures that will be brought to bear upon it by the arrival of the French Princess and her *escadron volante*.

Instead of continuing with his main action at this point, the playwright pursues his exposure of the imposture and hypocrisy of the gongoristic Armado. In the first scene he had a wit combat by proxy, with the natural wit of Costard triumphing over the artificial wit of the Spaniard. Now he wishes to show the conflict between Armado's false polished wit and the true sophisticated wit of the page Moth. The pretentiousness of the master's wit is no match for Moth's vivacious audacity. Where Costard had confounded Gongorism with literalness and a *reductio-ad-absurdum* simplicity, Moth meets Armado's pretentious lamentations with a deflating tautology that lures the susceptible Armado into foolish distinctions and feeble hair-splitting. Moth succeeds in turning every remark to his own advantage. He can ridicule his master's pretensions and call him a "cipher" to his face, but Armado is too vain and self-deluded to be aware of the contempt his pretensions have made him vulnerable to. When Armado looks for comfort in his love affair, he asks Moth what great men have been in love.

Moth. Hercules, master.

Arm. Most sweet Hercules! More authority, dear boy, name more. And, sweet my child, let them be men of good repute and carriage.

Moth. Samson, master. He was a man of good carriage, great carriage, for he carried the town gates on his back like a porter – and he was in love.

Arm. O well-knit Samson! Strong-jointed Samson! I do excel thee in my rapier as much as thou didst me in carrying gates. I am in love too. Who was Samson's love, my dear Moth?

Moth. A woman, master. (I.ii. 68-81)

In this combat between false and true wit, part of the humor arises from the use of the reversal-of-roles device. Here the master instead of being the dominant one is the submissive and tractable one, although he fancies himself in the former role. Instead of being in control of the situation, he is being manipulated like a puppet. Because of his self-deception and affectation, he is oblivious of the true state of affairs and sees himself as a Hercules or Samson in love, both of whom, ironically, were made fools of by women.

The same scene also brings him back into conflict with natural humor when Dull, Costard, and Jaquenetta enter. Even the simple, uncomplicated wench gets the best of him in their brief conversation. Her colloquial speech is misinterpreted by Armado and she mocks him with the simplest of irony, "Lord, how wise you are!"

In the exchange which follows, between Moth and Costard, we have a reversal of roles again. In his contest with Armado Moth had been the wit and his master the gull. We expect the page's wit and polish to do the same for him here, but he is undone by the rustic's malapropisms and *non sequiturs* and the two go off together with Costard having the last word, "I thank God I have as little patience as another man, and therefore I can be quiet".

The stage is left to Armado, and the departure of genuine wit is emphasized by the gongoristic soliloquy he closes the scene with,

I do affect the very ground, which is base, where her shoe, which is baser, guided by her foot, which is the basest, doth tread. I shall be forsworn, which is a great argument of falsehood, if I love. And how can that be true love which is falsely attempted? Love is a familiar, Love is a devil. There is no evil angel but Love. (I.ii. 172-178)

He brings his self-exposure to a climax with a comical, pseudo-heroic valedictory,

> Adieu, valor! Rust rapier! Be still, drum!
> For your manager is in love – yea, he loveth.
> Assist me, some extemporal god of rhyme, for
> I am sure I shall turn sonnet. Devise, wit;
> write, pen; for I am for whole volumes in
> folio. (I.ii. 186-191)

With such an occasion for sonneteering – an infatuation for a light wench – Armado exits, an object lesson in the folly of affectation.

The first act is a well structured one: its two scenes have been executed adroitly and swiftly. Scene i has handled the expository material of the B plot, which involves the romantic conflict between the King and his fellow celibates and the Princess and her entourage, who are coming to settle the old debt between France and Navarre. The blocking force in the central comic action, Ferdinand and his absurd compact, has been clearly delineated and its antagonist, the deprecating force of Berowne as the *eiron*, has been established as an ally of the moving force provided by the Princess and her ladies. Furthermore, the main characters and incidents of the C plot, the parodying subplot, and their relation to the main plot have been set up: Costard's dalliance with Jaquenetta sets up the first complication, and Armado's infatuation sets up the first intrigue.

Act I has succeeded in setting up the usurping or artificial society in the "little Academe" of Navarre. It is now the playwright's task to show the antithetical society and to lay the groundwork for the main action of the play which is to be based on the antagonism between the usurping and the legitimate society with the ultimate defeat and deposition of the former.

Act II falls far below the level of Act I structurally. For one thing, it is too short; for another, it lacks the balance provided by tonal contrast. It sets up a feeble internal complication in the B plot in the too ready capitulation of the blocking force, thus rendering subsequent action anti-climactic. Furthermore, there is too much talk and not enough dramatic complexity. The act contains only one scene, which is completely dominated by witty exchanges, where it should have had at least two, perhaps three, scenes to help create complications that would stimulate interest and suspense on several plot levels. These weaknesses arise from the playwright's not yet understanding the principle of coterminous action, which he does not master until he writes *A Midsummer Night's Dream*.

Shakespeare uses the Lylean device of symmetrical character groups to set up the lines of battle. The Princess is pitted against Navarre; Rosaline against Berowne; Maria against Longaville; and Katherine against Dumain. In the initial skirmish, the features of the young ladies are concealed by masks, placing the young men at a disadvantage by depriving them of the opportunity of seeing what each of the young ladies look like. This ambiguity of identities is a transparent device to permit the further confusion of identities which occurs later on in the play as a result of the machinations of the young ladies abetted by Boyet.

In this first contact between the warring societies, Boyet serves as the pivotal point about which the separate frays revolve. His is the spirit of worldly wisdom that smoothly expedites the inevitable association of young men with young women. His is a god-like role: that of an elder Cupid, as it were. He is a plot expediter and he operates through his role as liaison man between the two hostile camps. He not only serves to effect the first contact but also later helps to prolong the action by spying on the young men and informing the ladies of their plan to disguise themselves as Russians. He later confounds the performers in the masque and hastens the capitulation of Berowne.

He is also used to bring out one of the secondary themes in the play, namely, that beauty is purchased through tribute of the eyes and not by words. When he praises the Princess' beauty, she admonishes him that one falls in love not through the effect of words but through the physiological mechanism of sight, i.e., through a natural process not through a studied artifice of language. This physiological-psychological process is made possible by bringing the young lords into the presence of the young ladies so that they can be visually smitten despite all their resolve to the contrary.

In the conversation that occurs while Boyet is on his mission to the King, the young ladies engage in characterizations of the young lords. Longaville is represented by Maria as "a merry mocking" lord whose only defect is "a sharp wit matched with too blunt a will". Dumaine is depicted by Katherine as "a well-accomplished youth... For he hath wit to make an ill shape good, And shape to win grace though he had no wit." Rosaline in turn says of Berowne, "but a merrier man,/ Within the limits of becoming mirth/ I never spent an hour's talk withal". The outcome of the impending conflict is never seriously in doubt: the impossibility of the vows being kept is manifest. From these admiring descriptions and the obvious pairing off of young lady with young man, it is clear that the frigid restraint imposed by the oath will melt under the heart-warming glances exchanged between opponents.

Boyet returns from the court of Navarre with a declaration of open war. The King means to lodge the ladies in an open field "Like one that comes here to besiege his court". Ironically, this is exactly the situation that prevails: the young ladies, representing the forces of normal society, are at war with the young lords, the advocates of an "unnatural" society. As Caroline Spurgeon points out, the dominating symbolical imagery is that of war and weapons.

The main underlying theme of the confounding and dispelling of the fog of false idealism by the light of the experience of real life is presented through a series of brilliant encounters, when even the laughter 'stabs', the tongue is keen as 'the razor's edge invisible', and lets missiles fly to right and left— conceits having wings

> Fleeter than arrows, bullets, wind,
> thought, swifter things,

and words being pictured throughout as rapier-like thrusts, arrows, bullets fired from a cannon or as combatants tilting with their spears at a tournament. Longaville's wit is described as a sharp-edged sword handled by too blunt a will, Moth carries Armado's messages as a bullet from the gun, Boyet and Biron tilt straight and merrily at each other, Boyet's eye wounding 'like a leaden sword', while the jesting Biron, at the end, in despairing capitulation, stands in front of Rosaline and cries, lady, dart thy skill at me;

. . . .
Thrust thy sharp wit quite through
my ignorance
Cut me to pieces with thy keen conceit.[10]

When the ladies turn their clever wits on one another at the departure of the young lords, the Princess reminds them "This civil war of wits were much better used / On Navarre and his bookmen, for here 'tis abused."

The first battle of the war ends with the mock capitulation of Navarre and his lords. The next task of the dramatist is to provide the precipitating incidents whereby the capitulation is genuine, open, and irrevocable.

Act III, like Act II, is poorly executed from a dramatic standpoint: action is minimal and witty exchanges dominate the act without doing much to further complicate either the C plot, with which it is mostly concerned, or the B plot, which it turns to with the arrival of Berowne. Because of his insufficient command of the principle of coterminous action, the playwright has to treat the incidents in the different plots sequentially. In exactly the same number of lines (205) and at the same point in the play in *A Midsummer Night's Dream*, the more experienced playwright will effect the characterization of Bottom, the intrigue of Puck, the flight of the rude mechanicals, the infatuation of Titania for the "translated" Bottom, and the latter's delightful interchange with Masters Mustardseed, Cobweb, and Peaseblossom. In this early effort all he succeeds in doing is to provide topically allusive wordplay, superfluous from the standpoint of characterization and obstructive from the standpoint of plot movement.

In this act, he parodies this war of wits between the courtly lovers on the gongoristic level of the love smitten Armado bewailing his plight to Moth. The verbal play which was clever and amusing in its own right in the previous scene becomes amusing here primarily because of the satirical element in it. This is affectation being punctured, and the hapless Armado entertains us by virtue of his lack of wit not by any possession and skillful use of it.

---

[10] *Shakespeare's Imagery and What It Tells Us* (Cambridge, 1935), pp. 271-272.

To emphasize his pathetic pretensions he is always pitted against either the true, polished wit of Moth or the simple, rustic wit of Costard. In either case Armado always comes off a poor second, without ever being aware that he has been bested, so deep is his self-delusion and so shallow his perception.

In contrast to the witty exchanges between the ladies and between them and the young lords, the wit here is all one-sided. Moth's mental dexterity makes it possible for him to twist the most innocuous of Armado's remarks into a barb directed against the hapless Spaniard's bombast without the other being aware he has even been pricked. The page calls his master an ass and his lady a wanton and all the pompous master can say is, "A most acute juvenal, voluble and free of grace!"

Costard appears on the scene in answer to Armado's summons, providing another opportunity to display the supremacy of natural, unpolished wit over affected wit. Where Armado misuses the language because of his fanciful, figurative application of it and makes himself ridiculous in the process, Costard misuses it because of his canny literal application of it and overwhelms his adversary in the process. The word "enfranchise" becomes "one Francis", the words "immured, restrained, captivated, bound" become equated with the state of his bowels, and in a crowning feat of misapplication of language, the words "remuneration" and "guerdon" become equated with the tangible "three farthings" and "shilling". It is an amazing tour de force: the gongoristic Armado has been defeated at his own game. Operating on the level of high abstractions he has been bludgeoned by the literal language of Costard acting on the level of lowly concreteness. It is a fell blow that the badly defeated gongorism cannot hope to survive. It has met a dual defeat. It has been pierced by the rapier of true wit and clubbed by the homely staff of natural humor.

Throughout this central portion of the play, which should contain a series of rapidly occurring incidents leading to a climax, the playwright relies heavily on language as a structural device to create the atmosphere of affectation versus nature instead of using action to create suspense. As a result, he slows down the comic rhythm and fails to build any suspense, the equilibrium between expectation and surprise. When Armado and Moth engage in their wit bout, we are entertained momentarily but not further involved in any action which is part of a motivating complication or intrigue. The combat with Costard serves a more useful turn structurally in helping to propel the action forward through the device of the letter entrusted to the clown, but it is an extremely mild and suspenseless form of intrigue, one where expectation far outweighs surprise. The confessed apostasy of Berowne in his extravagant, oxymoronic eulogy of Rosaline is a dramatically inept attempt to complicate the B plot by a weakly contrived intrigue within its own element. In the absence of a D plot or a fully developed C plot, the playwright lacks the means to propel the action forward without resorting to static, non-suspenseful exposition, which is precisely what Berowne's speech is regardless of how entertaining it might be rhetorically as an elegant tonal contrast to the ludicrous gongorism of Armado. It is not exposition or further verbal pyrotechnics the playwright needs here but a cleverly interlocking multi-level plot structure.

Acts I and II had established the two rival societies and shown them in preliminary conflict. Act III furthered the action by showing the imminent capitulation of one representative of the usurping society. Now the dramatist has to make this surrender involve the entire society and prepare for the inevitable comic catastrophe. To accomplish this the playwright uses the multiple exposure scene borrowed from Lyly's *Gallathea* and the device of the misdelivered letters.

The hunting scene serves to provide an occasion for the misdelivery of Armado's letter to Rosaline and also to give occasion for further witty exchanges between the young ladies and Boyet. T. W. Baldwin makes much of the banter between the Princess and the forester concerning her twisting of his compliment "fair". He assigns a weighty significance to it in connection with the Protestant belief in "salvation by grace" as opposed to the Catholic one of "salvation by merit". He labors the point and insists that Shakespeare is labeling as heresy the doctrine of justification by works, and is applying that doctrine to beauty and merit.[11] From

---

[11] *Shakespeare's Five-Act Structure*, p. 598.

the general tone of the play it is highly problematical that the playwright was concerned with making such a solemn pronouncement. The remarks can stand on their own merits. The Princess is simply using her wit to chide the all-too-eager servitor for indulging in the conventional, meaningless compliments on her beauty, since her wit is adornment enough to be praised.

When Costard arrives, his literalness of language meets its match in the Princess' sophisticated use of the very device he uses naturally. She turns his "greatest lady" into "The thickest and the tallest". Instead of the polite deference of the royal forester she is treated with the refreshingly blunt observation of the rustic who assigns her a position of preëminence because she is the "thickest" present.

Costard, obligingly enough for the purposes of the slender plot, delivers the wrong letter. It is immediately recognized as one written by Armado to Jaquenetta, and provides much sport for the courtly critics. The language of the letter may very well be a parody of the style of some particular well-known figure of the day, but too much ink has already been spilled in inconclusive attempts to find the supposed original for Armado for a solution to be sought here. One does not need to know the precise original to be amused by the sight of affectation of language being coupled with affectation of feeling. The letter conveys perfectly the desired sense of pretended emotion larded over with repetitions, circumlocutions, empty comparisons, and total irrelevancies.

Again true wit is juxtaposed against the false wit of Armado's love letter in the badinage between Boyet and Rosaline. She carefully parries every *double entendre* of the old courtier but at the same time makes it quite clear that she is a woman ready to be loved by a man worthy of her mettle. On her departure Costard joins in the bawdy interchange and delivers an unconsciously fitting judgment on it in his,

> O' my troth, most sweet jests, most incony vulgar wit!
> When it comes so smoothly off, so obscenely, as it were, so fit.

Scene ii of Act IV provides the counterpart of action in scene i. Here the letter to Rosaline is mistakenly delivered to Jaquenetta.

At this point Holofernes and Nathaniel are brought into the play, quite extraneously from a structural standpoint but felicitously from a comic one. Holofernes serves as an object example of empty and pretended learning; Nathaniel, as the gullible, sycophantic follower of the bogus wise man. They are not essential to the plot but are maneuvered into it so that the playwright can furnish instances of deviation from the natural and the laughable folly it engenders. The pedantry of Holofernes is accentuated by a double foil: an admiring follower in Sir Nathaniel and a deflating antagonist in the rustic Dull whose obtuseness dulls the effect of Holofernes' cumbersome learning. Costard is used to deflate Armado with natural cleverness; Dull is used to deflate Holofernes with natural stupidity. In both instances there is a triumph of unpremeditated nature over studied effort, and the humor results from the reversal of roles. One would expect the conscious, studied opponent to triumph, but instead it is the unconscious, naive one that emerges victorious. Here Holofernes uses the language of ignorance wisely.

Holofernes and his crew are further useful as a structural device in that they provide the means whereby the two warring societies in the main plot can reconcile their differences and be allied in mirth at the expense of continuing affectation. The pageant of the Nine Worthies arranged by Holofernes affords the occasion for the reconciliation in mirth in the last act. The force of the laughter can now be directed away from the erstwhile celibate society to the gongoristic-pedantic-rustic society of Holofernes, Armado, and Costard.

The weakness in plot construction that started with Act II continues to the last scene in Act IV. The first two scenes of this act are simply transparent contrivances to get the letters misdelivered. The first scene is dominated by the wit of the Princess and her entourage and is essentially static; the second, by the verbal battle involving pedantry (Holofernes), sycophancy (Sir Nathaniel), and obtuseness (Dull), which has no real connection with the C plot and yet does not help for an independent D plot. Although the climactic mutual discovery scene is structurally the best in the play in its use of reversals, it comes too late and ends, not in action, but in an anticlimactic, movement-retarding speech which offers only vague promise of resolving the conflict in the B plot. At this point one might have legitimately expected a scene showing a climactic incident in the Armado-Jaquenetta-Costard love triangle or C plot, but nothing further is heard of it until Act V, and then it is merely alluded to as part of the general banter. One is forced to conclude that either the playwright was not concerned with constructing a complex but integrated plot or that he had not yet found the formula which would permit the synchronizing of disparate stories into a unified plot structure.

The linear action of the play, slender as it is, is brought to a climax in Act IV through a reversal-of-roles device: the apostate votaries to celibacy are now all doting lovers. They expose their defections to one another by a bit of stage business Shakespeare probably borrowed from Lyly's *Gallathea*. Berowne is the initial figure from which the denouement proceeds. Ironically, he is the first whose defection we become positively aware of, but he is the last to be exposed. He appears on the stage arguing with himself in the euphuistic vein of his soliloquy to "Dan Cupid", and steps aside when he sees the king entering reading from a paper in his hands. Navarre unburdens himself of amorous poetic sentiments to his lady-love, the Princess, and steps aside when Longaville arrives in similar straits. He divulges his love for Maria in a sugared sonnet, and in turn conceals himself at the arrival of Dumain. After eavesdropping on Dumain's lament, Longaville confronts him with a sanctimonious accusation of perjury. The King upbraids them both, and Berowne has a short-lived triumph over all three in a pretended innocence which is stripped away by the arrival of Costard with the letter Berowne had penned to Rosaline.

Thus, each in turn has experienced a comic reversal of fortune. From presumably contented celibacy, each has been catapulted into the ormented state of the lover. Each has also experienced a comic reversal of roles: from being the observer of his comrades' defection, he in turn becomes the observed, and from being the superior "innocent" one, he becomes the culprit. Each also experiences a reversal of intention. Each intends to recite his love poem in secret but succeeds in airing it to those he would most wish to conceal it from.

With all exposed as forswearers of their common oath, the task is now to reconcile their defection with their original promise. Berowne is selected as the attorney to prove that their loving is lawful and their fidelity not damaged. His speech at the end of this act is one to gratify the strongest scruple of those defending the "natural" or temporarily deposed society.

Despite their desire to return to the society of normal intercourse, the pseudo-celibates are not to be so easily exonerated of past guilt. They had made a solemn vow, and they must be punished for being so faithless to their word, no matter how foolish the vow. They must be humiliated by the defenders of the true society and be forced to admit openly they have renounced their guilty past. They must pay a price in order to gain re-admission to the "natural" society. That price will be the going awry of their love's labors and their consequent mortification.

This mortification is left for Act V to accomplish. Unfortunately, this act is a weak, over-long hodge-podge instead of a skillful bringing together of resolved complications. The only action in a quibble-filled first scene is the last-minute organization of the entertainment to be presented at court by Armado and his associates. Scene ii is an extremely long one (941 lines), yet all it accomplishes is the comically insipid routing of the false Muscovites and the presentation of the comic masque. Nothing is resolved by the inevitable operation of internal forces: resolution in the B plot depends on the abrupt arrival of a force from the A plot, and adequate resolution of the C plot is neglected entirely. Wordy episode and buffoonish spectacle substitute for carefully resolved structure.

Judging solely from the structure of the play one might reasonably assume that this is one of the earliest of Shakespeare's comic efforts. It certainly suffers from a number of structural deficiencies. A thinly contrived main plot inadequately supported by an incompletely resolved subplot forms the basis of a relatively uneventful story. The piece exists more for the sake of displaying verbal brilliance than for any sustained developing of comic conflict. The action never moves forward with any real sense of intriguing complications leading to an inevitable climax. The various comic reversals – of intention, of fortune, and of roles – are in themselves amusing occasionally, but they are not yet being used in a crescendo-like manner to attain the maximum effect. The catastrophe in the B plot seems lamely arrived at, and the playwright resorts to a *deus ex machina* to resolve his plot rather than by arranging an inevitable concurrence of events that tie the enveloping action or the parodying subplot in with the main action.

Perhaps, as Charlton suggests, this should not be regarded as a real play but more as an exercise in the play of words. "It is the work of a poet who was born into an age of drama, – but as yet is only vaguely cognizant of the demands of drama as distinct from those of poetry."[12] The young poet trying his hand at stagecraft is too enamoured of the sound of words and delights too much in his clever manipulating of language until it bends to his every need except that of plot movement. Every verbal trap – gongoristic bombast, pedantic nonsense, bawdy wordplay, and clownish malapropisms – attracts him at the price of sound dramatic structure. They are often clever examples of word manipulation, but they are not used in a sufficiently integrated manner to weave character and plot together. They too often exist for their own sake because they are sparkling proof of the young poet's verbal dexterity rather than because they perform a structural function.

But this is not the type of play a practical dramatist can go on writing indefinitely. Lyly had gained his reputation as a court playwright with exactly this type of slender dramatic fare, but it was going out of popularity by the time Shakespeare wrote this play. It is not mere verbal brilliance that builds great drama – comedy or tragedy. Diction is only one of the elements of drama, and no matter how brilliant it may be, it is still properly only one of the lesser elements. It must be subordinated to the interests of character and plot, or at least not be permitted to override them as so often happens in this play. As yet the young playwright has not disciplined his genius to the difficult task of underplaying one's chief asset and developing elements which may have to be learned by

[12] *Shakespearian Comedy* (New York, 1938), pp. 100-102.

hard study rather than coming easily by nature. Poetry and wit come easily for this talented writer, but dramatic structure is presently something he is not quite so adept in. He must subject himself to further schooling in the architectonics of comedy even if it means temporarily neglecting his more natural talents.

The comic elements that are to be found in his mature works are developed only embryonically in this present play. The playwright is inexpertly attempting to handle repeated ironic reversals, but he succeeds only in creating vignettes not a sustained comic structure. The Costards and the Dulls have to reach full maturity and develop their own separate C plot with carefully worked out complications and an inevitable resolution related to one of the other plots before Shakespeare's efforts will reach the heights of great comedy. The Berownes and Rosalines will have to develop real characters of their own rather than being mere mouthpieces for witticisms before they will become genuinely humorous and appealing in their own right. The beginning is here; it is simply a matter of careful development and further breaking away from the limiting artifice of Master John Lyly.

III. *THE TWO GENTLEMEN OF VERONA*

As with *Love's Labour's Lost* and *The Comedy of Errors* the precise date of composition and first performance of *The Two Gentlemen of Verona* has not been satisfactorily established, leaving the structural analyst with no exact sequence for the early plays to help him in the study of Shakespeare's development from tyro to master in the difficult art of stagecraft. That this is a novice work, written early in the dramatist's career, is beyond cavil; it has been variously estimated as having been first performed anywhere between 1591 and 1595. Although it is mentioned in Meres' list of 1598, no text of the play exists earlier than that of the First Folio. This interesting fact probably indicates that the play was never popular enough to be worthwhile pirating in quarto form or to be worth legitimate printing by the playwright's agent in order to combat pirating or capitalize on any interest the play might have inherited from frequent performances on the public stage. Another singular feature about the publication history of the play is that the Folio edition omits all stage directions and contains few indications for entrances and exits within the scenes. This almost complete absence of managerial directions would lend support to the conjecture that the play was a failure on the stage and was not performed often enough to deserve careful attention being paid to keeping an accurate acting copy in the company's files.

In *Love's Labour's Lost* Shakespeare had emphasized speech at the expense of action. In this play, however, the action in the B plot is skilfully complicated and brought to a climax, and language is used functionally to propel the play forward, not primarily to entertain by its wit and beauty. Viewed in detail from a structural standpoint, the play still shows weaknesses that suggest that the playwright had not yet solved certain basic problems of motivation, multi-level action, atmosphere, and tone. Even though *Love's Labour's Lost* sacrifices dramatic action to verbal pyrotechnics, its C plot offers a more satisfactory parody, and the tone and atmosphere support the slender story better than those elements do in this play. Furthermore, Armado and Costard are better characterized and more skillfully integrated with the B plot than are the C plot principals in this presumably later play. If *The Two Gentlemen of Verona* actually is a later play, it would indicate that in Shakespeare's development as a dramatist growth was not steady but rather uneven, depending on which element he was giving his attention to.

Despite its own generally acknowledged dramatic deficiencies and its apparent lack of success in the theater, the play does provide patterns of incidents and characters which are used later on when the dramatist has solved the structural problems he is only experimenting with in his play. The plight of a young maiden who has an unwanted suitor forced on her by a stern father opposed to the suitor of her choice is used again in Juliet's ill-starred love. The famous balcony scene in the later tragedy of young love is clearly presaged in the mention of Silvia's tower window, accessible only by a perilous climb. So also does the playwright use the device of banishment of the hero again, not only in *Romeo*, but also in *As You Like It*. Julia seeks advice on her suitors from her confidante and go-between, Lucetta, in a scene pointing to the much more adroitly handled one in *The Merchant of Venice*, where Portia puts Nerissa to a similar use. Julia, in quest of her lover, dons the garb of a boy as do her more famous literary sisters, Rosalind and Viola. What this demonstrates is that the playwright built his crowning achievements on the ground cleared by his earlier efforts.

Very much the same sort of thing can be said of *Love's Labour's Lost*, in which Costard and the other Worthies prefigure the rude mechanicals of *A Midsummer Night's Dream:* Berowne and Rosaline, the more brilliant Benedick and Beatrice; and Holofernes and Nathaniel, the comedy pair of Sir Toby Belch and Sir Andrew Aguecheek.

All that these self-owed debts prove is that the artist was to do more successfully later on what he never quite succeeds in doing well here or in the other two early comedies: create memorable characters whose relation to the comic action is a genuinely functional one. Even though these early efforts are comparative failures, one can see, blessed by the hindsight conferred by the dramatist's later works, that he is grappling with the right problems. The apprentice dramatist as yet lacks the theatrical skill to fashion a slender plot of his own or a loosely spun tale and a highly idealized theme into a skilfully coördinated dramatic structure demonstrating a firm grasp of the concept of ironic reversals operating on different levels but producing a single effect.

The loosely spun tale and the highly idealistic theme Shakespeare employs in this play came to him through Renaissance modifications of the medieval romance. The plot of the play corresponds in its main features with the story of the formidable huntress Felismena in the Spanish prose pastoral romance *Diana Enamorada* by Jorge de Montemayor. The exact manner in which Shakespeare became familiar with the story is not known. He may have had access to a manuscript copy of Bartholomew Yonge's English translation of the Spanish romance or he may have read a French version by Nicholas Colin which was available in England about the time the play was most likely written. It is even possible he may have witnessed a performance of or read an earlier dramatic version of the story in a lost play, *Felix and Philomena*, reputedly acted before the Queen at Greenwich in 1584.[1]

Julia in Shakespeare's play corresponds to the faithful Felismena in the de Montemayor romance. Felix, the erring lover of Felismena, is the original of Proteus. The courtship of Felix and Felismena plays a much more extensive part in the Spanish tale, but the English dramatist retains its cardinal features. The scene in which Lucetta brings Proteus' letter to her mistress follows closely the scene in the original. In fact, the playwright employs most of the scenes and actions appearing in the narrative. Proteus, like Felix, is sent to court; Julia, like Felismena, follows him disguised

---

[1] Frederick S. Boas, *Shakespeare and his Predecessors* (New York, 1905), p. 190.

as a boy. She too overhears her lover propose to a rival, takes service as a page with her false lover, is sent as a messenger to the rival lady, describes the beauty of the jilted lady, etc. The playwright does make changes in the main story, however, to suit the purposes of comedy. He splits the character of Felix in two by the creation of Valentine as a counterpart to the rival lady so that there will be a brace of couples, thereby ensuring a happy ending instead of a mournful one for the rival lady. By this character division he also provides a basis for the ruptured friendship theme which is nowhere to be found in the Spanish pastoral. There the rival lady had fallen in love with the page, as Shakespeare later has Olivia fall in love with Viola, and died of unrequited love. In the play Shakespeare has Silvia, the rival lady, only deeply pity the rejected lady and form a friendship with the tender-hearted page. The means whereby the dramatist effects a reconciliation between his estranged lovers bears no relation to the resolution in the *Diana*.

Rather than inventing these divergencies from de Montemayor, Shakespeare may have merely borrowed from another source. Again, as with the stock figures of the pedant, braggart, and parasite in *Love's Labour's Lost*, he may have borrowed the characters and the situation of the false friend from Italian comedy. In *Flavio Tradito*, a play in Flaminio Scala's book of collected scripts published in 1611, Oratio proves false to his sworn friend Flavio by making love to Isabella, Flavio's loved one. Flavio eventually learns of Oratio's perfidy but does not take action immediately. One day, Flavio, discovering his friend about to be slain in a duel, magnanimously rushes to his rescue. At this gesture of sincere friendship, Oratio, overcome by remorse for his infidelity, surrenders Isabella to Flavio, and the damaged friendship is restored to its pristine beauty. The similarity between this play and the ending in Shakespeare's is so marked that one must accept his debt either to this very play or to the general tradition of ideal courtly friendship of which it is a representative. In this highly conventionalized type of Italian comedy, theme is allowed to dominate over character and plot to the extent that probability is severely wrenched, and character never develops beyond the stock figures of the true-lover-and-friend, the false-lover-and-friend, and the innocent and true lady-love-in-between who is merely a pawn in the contest of who is the more devoted friend. The young English dramatist apparently permitted himself to be guided by the necessities dictated by the theme than by those of dramatic characterization and motivation.

As a part of its idealized, courtly theme, the play exhibits many of the conventions of *fine amor*, the love code of chivalry which prevailed from the twelfth to the sixteenth century, and the *hereos* or illness from which the lover of romance was supposed to suffer.[2] Speed, for example, derides his master for being in love and going ungartered just as the latter had earlier chided Proteus for his love-sickness.

Val. Why, how know you that I am in love?
Speed. Marry, by these special marks: first, you have learned, like Sir Proteus, to wreathe your arms like a malcontent; to relish a love-song, like a robin-redbreast; to walk alone, like one that had the pestilence; to sigh, like a school-boy that had lost his A B C; to weep, like a young wench that had buried her grandam; to fast, like one that takes diet; to watch, like one that fears robbing, to speak puling, like a beggar at Hallowmass. You were wont when you laugh'd, to crow like a cock; when you walk'd, to walk like one of the lions; when you fasted, it was presently after dinner; when you looked sadly, it was for want of money: and now you are metamorphos'd with a mistress, that, when I look on you, I can hardly think you are my master.   (II.i. 18-32)

Thus Valentine pays for his previous "contemning of Love" by his suffering when he falls in love with Silvia. He is punished with "bitter fasts" and loss of sleep, two very common afflictions of the melancholy lover.

According to the traditions of *fine amor* the lovers also make use of go-betweens and confidants. Speed plays the latter role mockingly in the scene quoted above, and Proteus employs the disguised Julia as his go-between to Silvia after he has discharged the clown Launce, who had earlier served him in that capacity. Lucetta, the servant to Julia, also serves as her confidante and go-between. As we have already seen, she advises her mistress as to which of the suitors to favor, and she brings Julia a letter which Speed has given her from Proteus.

[2] William Meader, *Courtship in Shakespeare* (New York, 1954), p. 7.

The play also follows the *fine amor* tradition relating to rings and other gifts. Julia's gift of a ring to Proteus is regarded by both as a token of espousal *de futuro*, and his giving it to Silvia is one of the serious evidences of his infidelity. Portraits, on the other hand, are not regarded as seriously in the tradition. The giving of a picture was much less significant of emotional commitment than the giving of a ring. Its conferring did not necessarily imply love, although the requesting and accepting of one seemed to have done so. Proteus in his treacherous pursuit of Silvia asks for her portrait even though she protests firmly that his suit is unwanted and hopeless. Even though she is far from encouraging his courtship, she still agrees to give him her picture because, according to convention, it is no admission of anything on her part nor any assumption of obligation that Proteus might legitimately hold her to later.[3]

The terms of endearment in the play also accord with the conventions of the courtly love tradition, which from the days of the Provençal poets considered the woman as the superior one in the love relationship. Accordingly, Valentine addresses Silvia as "mistress" and she calls him "servant".

According to the tradition, unless the union is sanctioned by one or both of the parents of the lovers, the plans have to be made by the lovers themselves. If the parents are in active opposition, plans for elopement are made in deep secrecy, shared only by the confidants, who usually assist in the preparations and actual flight. In this play, Valentine confides his plans to his supposedly loyal friend, Proteus, telling him that he intends to scale the wall to Silvia's high window with a rope-ladder that he will conceal on his person and carry his love off despite her father's opposition and contrary plans.

Added to this theme of *fine amor* dating back to the conventions of lady-worship of the high Middle Ages is the Renaissance one of idealized friendship between two courtiers. The Renaissance courtier had an elaborate code of conduct prescribed for him and a formidable list of virtues he had to aspire toward and achieve. From the translators of Castiglione to Spenser, gentleman-writers in

[3] Meader, pp. 138-139.

England held before the Elizabethan courtier the high ideals he owed fealty to. Not only did he read about them and hear them discoursed upon at length, he also saw them exemplified in paragons such as Sir Philip Sidney, the living embodiment of the courtly ideal. The virtues of the ideal courtier included first of all, as a part of Justice, the golden attribute of Fidelity or Constancy. Proteus' name immediately singles him out as a defector from the cardinal gentlemanly virtue. When he begs for forgiveness of his sins from his virtuous friend Valentine, the latter in granting forgiveness is merely displaying in its ultimate form the courtly ideal of Magnanimity which, as in Spenser's Prince Arthur, is the sum total of all courtly virtues. The magnanimous courtier ignored wrong done to him and forgave his malefactors freely. He sought always to confer benefits rather than receive them, as exemplified by Sidney declining the drink of water on the battlefield in favor of the wounded soldier even though he himself was mortally stricken.

In order to understand the play one has to be aware of these two traditions: the medieval one of *fine amor* and the Renaissance one of ideal friendship. If the actions of the play are judged against the standards of common sense and normal behavior, they become incomprehensible and lead to the irrelevant moral strictures passed on the play by Victorian critics, who saw in Valentine's deeding of Silvia to Proteus an example of total moral depravity. Such critics were simply not aware of the governing fact that Valentine is acting according to Renaissance idealism, not according to the probabilities of human behavior governing the actions of a young man "in love" in the modern sense of the word. Valentine has to be recognized as the personification of the ideal courtly friend for whom no sacrifice or surrender is too great so long as it be in the sacred name of friendship.

Recognizing the ideological background of the play and the conventions that shape its action is not the same, however, as saying that it is a well-constructed stage piece. The material is too refractory to be adapted to the Elizabethan popular stage without some extensive alterations being made first. These alterations have not been made, however, because at this point in his irregular progress the playwright does not seem to have a sufficiently well developed sense of comic conflict. Structurally, the play cries out for an *alazon*, like Duke Ferdinand in *Love's Labour's Lost*, who is the proponent of a false society and who is being attacked by an *eiron*, like Berowne, who voices the prejudices of the audience and their resistance to the false tenets of the would-be usurping society. In this play, the B plot is composed entirely of *alazons*. The *eirons* from the C plot, Launce and Speed, are not developed enough dramatically to serve in a sustained ironic parody of the main plot: for one thing, they lack a Jaquenetta or an Audrey as a counterpart to the romantic heroine. Shakespeare has too readily accepted the values of his *alazons*, whose true comic role he is not yet aware of, and does not exploit them as fit sources of humor. They are shielded by an impossibly idealized code from the salutary influence of laughter which would convert them to the ways of the "normal" society represented by the audience-surrogate, the *eiron*.

For these reasons the theory that this play is a deliberate parody[4] of the conventions of the romance tradition does not seem to be a tenable one. Rather than being a sophisticated outsider the play-wright seems to be more the naive insider. If this parody theory were the correct appraisal of the tone and purpose of the play, there would have been an *eiron* in the B plot to serve as the standard against which the ridiculous could be measured, or the C plot would have been developed in greater detail to emphasize the folly, if such it was intended to be, of the actions in the B plot. The playwright's preoccupation with the B plot to the virtual neglect of the other potential plots would seem to indicate that he was interested in it for its own sake but simply could not handle it as effectively as he wished. If it had been parody, Valentine and Proteus would have been rendered laughable in the conventionalized resolution scene by having their purposes crossed, but there is no indication of this at all. Rather than a deliberate parody, it would seem more likely that it is only an unconscious one brought about by the ineptness of the playwright in attempting to handle refractory material.

Besides being conditioned by elements from medieval romance and Renaissance philosophy, the play is also influenced by ritualistic elements that tie it in with the medieval tradition of the seasonal

4 H. C. Goddard, *The Meaning of Shakespeare* (Chicago, 1951), pp. 42-46.

ritual play. Frye calls a play of this type "the drama of the green world",[5] its plot being associated with the ritual theme of the triumph of life over sterility and death. The action of such a play begins in a world represented as the ordinary workaday world, moves into the "green world", undergoes a metamorphosis there in which the resolution of the action is effected, and returns finally to the sphere of mundane events. The forest of this play is a sparser version of the fairy world of *A Midsummer Night's Dream* and an embryonic one of the idyllic pastoral forest in *As You Like It*. All these "green world" comedies exhibit the same alternation between the ordinary "gray" world and the magic "green" one. This second world, or world of enchantment, is found only in Shakespeare's romantic comedies, being absent from the ironic ones like *Measure for Measure* and *All's Well That Ends Well*. This "green world" charges the romantic comedies with the symbolism of the victory of spring over winter, as is explicitly represented in the anti-masque ending of *Love's Labour's Lost*, where the play closes with a song and dance fashioned after the medieval *débats* between spring, the symbol of fertility and life, and winter, the symbol of sterility and death.

The difficulty in this play arises not from the use of a ritualistic element in the plot, but from a failure to exploit it fully, as the playwright later does in *A Midsummer Night's Dream* and *As You Like It*, where magic of the forest is carried to its highest dramatic use. Without the willing suspension of disbelief enlisted by magic, the events in this play become merely weakly motivated incredibilities relying on idealistic conventions for their acceptance by the audience. With the addition of forest magic, these same actions become engaging youthful excesses in the playwright's later triumphs in romantic comedy. Without the supra-rational and the kaleidoscope of magic to diffuse a softer light on them, the actions of the lovers in this too-real forest between Milan and Mantua become simply trivial improbabilities. The playwright has not yet learned how to cast the mantle of acceptability on basically improbable events. The device used in this play, the forest outlaws who conveniently immobilize all the principal characters of the B plot

[5] Frye, pp. 181-184.

in one spot at one time, is palpably an ineptly used *deus ex machina*, not an integrated part of a multi-level plot with the bandits being part of a complicating and resolving D plot. "Neither before nor after *The Two Gentlemen of Verona* has dramatic literature known a band of outlaws like to these – except once: there are the Pirates of Penzance; but then Gilbert meant his to be funny."[6] The trip to the "green world" may look here as though the playwright has got himself lost in the woods, but actually he has returned with a pocketful of dramatic acorns that will yield the magic oaks of Arden and the woods of Athens.

A summary of the plot of this initial venture into the "green world" shows how sorely in need of the world of fancy is this combination of romance and comedy. The lovers occupy the center of the action without showing the genuine passion necessary to elevate their doings to any real level of interest. In the absence of genuine passion, they deserve a subordinate role; the B plot should be minimized, but the playwright does not do this as he later does with the actions of Hermia and Lysander, Helen and Demetrius. At this stage of his development, he puts romantic narrative into a loose dramatic form and appends to it the title "comedy" primarily because he has managed to contrive a happy ending and has comic interludes with his clowns adding merriment to the general proceedings but nothing to the development of a multi-level structure. These clowns are not true participants in a dramatic action; they are essentially *bomolochoi* or partakers of the general festivity. The contrived happy ending is reached by the most precipitous concatentation of absurd events unalleviated by any skillful ordering of final scenes based on the repetition of comic reversals or deflation of the pseudo-heroic, although he approaches the latter device timidly in the actions of Sir Thurio.

The play takes its name from the two chief male characters, Valentine and Proteus, two young gentlemen of Verona platonically devoted to one another. Valentine, ("true lover"), resolved to seek honor and preferment at the court of Milan, takes leave of his friend Proteus, ("changeable one"). The latter remains behind in Verona to pursue a budding love-affair with Julia, a much sought-

6   Charlton, p. 40.

after young gentlewoman of that city. Just when he has made progress in his wooing, his father, influenced by the example of Valentine's father, decides to send his own son to court to improve his prospects instead of wasting his time at home in idle pursuits.

In Milan it is now Valentine's turn to be smitten by the beauty of a young woman. The young lady who has him in thrall is Silvia, the daughter of the Duke of Milan. It is she who is the aggressive one in the wooing, commissioning Valentine to write love-letters for her to a "friend". She returns these letters to him in person with the request that they be written more movingly. He is informed by his servant Speed that the letters are really intended for him. But his happy union with Silvia is obstructed by the Duke's plans to match her with Sir Thurio, a suitor eligible because of his wealth and social position.

Back in Verona, Proteus has taken his enforced farewell of Julia to whom he has sworn eternal constancy in an exchange of rings. On his arrival in Milan, Valentine greets him lovingly, boasts of Silvia's rare beauty, discloses his plans for elopement, and enlists his friend's loyalty and assistance. Proteus, however, is also smitten by the beauty of Silvia, so much so that he completely forgets about his vows of fidelity to Julia and his obligation of undying loyalty to his friend. To clear the way for his own wooing of Silvia, he plans to betray his trusting friend's secret to the Duke. Meanwhile, Julia, unable to remain long separated from her "true" love, dons the costume of a boy and leaves Verona in search of her lover.

The faithless Proteus betrays the secret of the impending elopement to Silvia's father. Upon learning the news, the Duke seeks out Valentine, tricks him into telling him about the rope-ladder under the pretext that he needs one for his own wooing, and then punishes the young man by banishing him from the duchy. Now that Valentine has been removed as an obstacle to the fulfilment of his own desires, Proteus pursues his illicit courtship by pretending to aid the courtship of the fatuous Thurio.

In flight from the Duke's wrath, Valentine is waylaid by a band of brigands who inhabit the nearby forest. They are so impressed by their captive's manly beauty that they enlist him into their ranks as their leader. In Milan, Proteus continues his suit of Silvia, all the while pretending to be the go-between and confidant of Sir Thurio. In the midst of this intrigue, Julia arrives in Milan, takes lodgings in an inn, and overhears her faithless lover serenading another woman. Julia seeks and gains employment as a page to her fickle lover and is immediately despatched by him on an errand to Silvia to give her the very ring he had received from Julia in pledge of their love. The unwavering Silvia refuses the gift and in talking to the supposed page learns something of the wronged Julia.

To follow after the banished Valentine, Silvia flees Milan in company with Sir Eglamour, a devoted servitor of Love. The brigands capture her, but she is rescued by Proteus and the page. Proteus woos her ardently and threatens physical conquest to overcome her resistance. He is overheard by Valentine, who chances to be in a nearby cave. The grievously wronged lover and friend makes his presence known, and the false lover and friend bows down and begs his forgiveness. The magnanimous Valentine forgives his erring friend and even confers all his interest in the lady Silvia on the repentant friend. At this blow to her hopes, Julia faints and her true identity becomes known. In the midst of this confusion, the Duke and Thurio, also taken captive by the bandits, are brought before Valentine, the outlaw chieftain. Thurio refuses to fight for the hand of a woman who does not love him, and the Duke then confers his daughter's hand on Valentine. Proteus and Julia are now free to re-unite; the brigands are all pardoned; and the entire assembly returns happily to Milan, all wrongs righted, all problems, present and future, solved.

A structural analysis of the play surprisingly shows more evidence of dramatic skill than one might suppose from this series of accidents and incredibilities. Structurally the play can be considered as one of developing action, leading to complications of intrigue and irony, which is resolved through the agency of an extrinsic factor and which ends in a state of equilibrium. The subplot provides an atmosphere of earthy levity to parody the romantic seriousness of the main action. The opening situation is a complex one but one with no lines of comic conflict immediately apparent. The dramatist has structured three interests which are initially independent of one another: the platonized friendship of Valentine and Proteus, "the two gentlemen of Verona"; the love of one of them, Proteus, for Julia; and in Milan, the piece of social matchmaking involving Silvia, her father the Duke, and the favored suitor, Sir Thurio.[7]

The impetus for the first complication in the action arises from physical movement, that of Valentine to Milan. Plot movement, then, is initially dependent on spatial movement. Valentine's arrival in Milan initiates the first phase of the complicating action by his falling in love with Silvia and having his love reciprocated. Here we have the first line of comic conflict drawn, one that goes back to Greek and Roman comedy: the young lovers are opposed by the will of the *senex* and by the favored courtship of a wealthy rival for the young lady's hand. Unfortunately, however, this conflict is never developed along comic lines: it pursues a romantic course from beginning to end and never contributes to the laughter except indirectly and unintentionally. The Duke and Sir Thurio are never developed adequately as comic blocking figures representing a false society that has to be overcome. This love of Valentine for Silvia becomes the basis of an intrigue, since it must be concealed from the hostile eyes of the father and the favored suitor. This intrigue, in turn, leads to further complications: it lays the groundwork for the reversals of role and of fortune in the scene where Proteus betrays his friend's secret in the second complication of the developing action. Valentine's movement to Milan is also the motive force for the complicating action in the Proteus-Julia complex: it provides an ironic motivating circumstance for the physical separation and emotional alienation of these two lovers and the intrigues which result therefrom.

The second impetus for complicating the action comes from a second physical transplantation. This time it is the movement of Proteus which acts as the force. Actually his movement is a derivative of the first movement, that of Valentine to Milan. Like the first movement, this also sets up the stage for an intrigue, only this time a more involved one. First of all, there is the intrigue in love: Proteus must keep his disloyal infatuation for Silvia a secret until he has removed or circumvented the obstacles to his success.

[7] R. G. Moulton, *The Moral System of Shakespeare* (New York, 1907), pp. 222-228.

Secondly, there is an intrigue in friendship: Proteus must devise a means to deceive and undo his most intimate friend to whom he is supposedly bound by ties of undying loyalty. Finally, there is an intrigue against the social conventions governing courtship and marriage: Proteus pretends to be serving the interests of the legitimate suitor but is actually working in his own interests thereby deceiving the suitor, the father, and the young lady. Proteus is well aware of this threefold intrigue and he brings it to the attention of the audience.

> Already have I been false to Valentine
> And now I must be as unjust to Thurio.
> Under the color of commending him,
> I have access my own love to prefer.
> But Silvia is too fair, too true, too holy,
> To be corrupted with my worthless gifts.
> When I protest true loyalty to her,
> She twits me with my falsehood to my friend;
> When to her beauty I commend my vows,
> She bids me think how I have been forsworn
> In breaking faith with Julia whom I loved;
> And notwithstanding all her sudden quips,
> The least whereof would quell a lover's hope,
> Yet, spaniel-like, the more she spurns my love,
> The more it grows, and fawneth on her still.   (IV,ii. 1-15)

In the third complication impetus is again provided by physical movement: this time that of Julia to Milan in the guise of a boy. This movement produces a situation of multiple ironic reversals accruing from the multiple intrigue. The intrigue in love on the part of Julia and the one on the part of Proteus produce the reversal of fortune in which Julia overhears her false lover singing a serenade not to her, his legitimate love, who is present on the scene, but to an ineligible and unwilling rival.

Host. Now, young guest, methinks you're allycholy. I pray you, why is it?

Jul. Marry, mine host, because I cannot be merry.

Host. Come, we'll have you merry. I'll bring you where you shall hear music and see the gentleman that you ask'd for.

Jul. But shall I hear him speak?

Host. Ay, that you shall.

Jul. That will be music.   (Music plays)

Host.   Hark, hark!

Jul.   Is he among these?

Host.   Ay; but peace! let's hear 'em.

Song.

Who is Silvia? What is she,

.   .   .   .

To her let us garlands bring.

Host. How now! are you sadder than you were before: How do you, man? The music likes you not.

Jul.   You mistake; the musician likes me not.

Host. Why, my pretty youth?

Jul.   He plays false, father.

Host. How? Out of tune on the strings?

Jul.   Not so; but yet so false that he grieves my very heart strings.

Host. You have a quick ear.

Jul.   Ay, I would I were deaf; it makes me have a slow heart. (IV.ii. 26-61)

There is also an ironic reversal of intention in the friendship relationship in that Proteus serves to effect a rapport between Silvia and Julia which counterbalances the ruptured friendship between him and Valentine.

Jul.   Madam, he sends your ladyship this ring.

Sil.   The more shame for him that he sends it me; For I have heard him say a thousand times
His Julia gave it him at his departure.
Though his false finger have profan'd the ring,
Mine shall not do his Julia so much wrong.

Jul.   She thanks you.

Sil.   What say'st thou?

Jul.   I thank you, madam, that you tender her.
Poor gentlewoman! My master wrongs her much.

.   .   .   .

Sil.   She is beholding to thee, gentle youth.
Alas, poor lady, desolate and left!
I weep myself to think upon thy words.
Here youth, there is my purse; I give thee this
For thy sweet mistress' sake, because thou lov'st her.
Farewell.

Jul.   And she shall thank you for't, if e'er you know her.
A virtuous gentlewoman, mild and beautiful! (IV.iv. 137-185)

An ironic reversal of roles results from the social intrigue of Proteus.

By the gulling of the legitimate suitor, Sir Thurio, the go-between, Proteus, is allowed to assume the role of actual lover suing in his own behalf. Julia, paradoxically, is used in her office of page as an accomplice of Proteus to underline the irony of the situation in the asides she makes commenting on the inanity of Sir Thurio.

Thu. Sir Proteus, what says Silvia to my suit?
Pro. O, sir, I find her milder than she was; And yet she takes exceptions at your person.
Thu. What, that my leg is too long?
Pro. No; that it is too little.
Thu. I'll wear a boot, to make it somewhat rounder.
Jul. (Aside) But love will not be spurr'd to what it loathes.
Thu. What says she to my face?
Pro. She says it is a fair one.
Thu. Nay, then the wanton lies; my face is black.
Pro. But pearls are fair; and the old saying is, Black men are pearls in beauteous ladies' eyes.
Jul. (Aside) 'Tis true; such pearls as put out ladies' eyes.
For I had rather wink than look on them.
Thu. How likes she my discourse?
Pro. Ill, when you talk of war.
Thu. But well, when I discourse of love and peace?
Jul. (Aside) But better, indeed, when you hold your peace. (V.ii. 1-18)

In order to resolve the multiple intrigue and to dissipate the multiple irony, the dramatist has recourse to another physical movement, one which produces a re-alignment of characters. This is accomplished through the movement effected by the banishment of Valentine, a movement which was initiated by the intrigue of Proteus against friendship. But physical movement has taken the dramatist as far as he can go: movement must now be halted by a blocking force which brings about the resolution. Valentine must be stopped, and so also must all of those who follow in the wake of his banishment: Silvia and Sir Eglamour, Proteus and the page (Julia), the Duke and Sir Thurio. This stopping force is provided by the outlaws. They stop Valentine and incorporate him into the stopping force and are finally absorbed into and neutralized by the last moving force so that a state of equilibrium results. They also furnish the occasion for the leaving of the "green" world to return to the "ordinary" one.

The sustained irony of the plot thus intensifies to the point where the moving and stopping forces meet, and new combinations, or more properly the old ones, result: the faithful Julia wins back a repentant Proteus; Silvia and Valentine are reunited; and the outlaws return to Milan under ducal amnesty. At this point the, irony fades into pure romance. Just before this point is reached, the action has Proteus forcing his unwanted attentions on the protesting Silvia, who is apparently helpless in the forest but ironically is within range of her true love's protection. This ultimate breach of friendship and love leads ironically to a healing of the rupture. This healing involves a conferring of Silvia on Proteus by the forgiving Valentine; but this action in turn causes Julia to swoon and, by so doing, reveal her true identity. By some subtle alchemy of romance this restores her claim on Proteus, and Valentine and Silvia are left to pair off. The only remaining obstacle to this, Sir Thurio, ironically declines the favored position accorded him by the Duke. Valentine wins by default and he and Silvia are reunited. The intrigue and irony is all behind them.

From the above analysis, it can be seen that the novice has devised a creditable scheme of interlocking actions following a neat and balanced pattern, but he has used physical movement as his main propelling and unifying force to the almost complete exclusion of characterization and plausible motivation. Things happen because people are brought together by the exigencies of the story not because their characters are so structured that what they do is determined by what they are. He has succeeded in constructing a good set of plot complications, but it is a house of cards, supported by the props of accident and the guy-wires of convention, which topples to the ground in the forced agitation of a hastily contrived resolution.

This structural analysis would indicate that when Shakespeare wrote this play, he was aware that audiences like a crowded and complicated story. To satisfy this desire, he provides this involved plot based on multiple intrigue and multiple ironic reversals. He even attempts hesitantly to parody it with a clownish subplot. But involved as this scheme is, it still shows that he is at the beginning of his dramatic development. He is aware of the necessity of contrast and counterbalance, and he alternates his scenes of romance and comedy in order to achieve this. Sometimes he even splits scenes down the middle to attain this tonal contrast as in Act I, scene i where a serious conversation between Valentine and Proteus is followed by a verbal quibble of equal length that takes place between Proteus and Speed. The difficulty is that these contrasts are too obvious and too overdone. They are thrown in because he needs them rather than being made an integral part of the plot. Launce's lecture to his shoes in Act II, scene iii is amusing in itself, but it is a comic interlude rather than an intrinsic element of the plot.

Shakespeare's awkwardness in handling tonal contrast is matched by his ineptitude in providing expository material. At this stage in the development of his dramatic technique he requires ten scenes sprawled over two whole acts to set up the relations between the main participants in the action: Valentine with Proteus, Proteus with Julia, Valentine with Silvia, and Launce and Speed with one another and with the others. This stringing out of static expository material and transitional scenes seriously impedes the tempo of the play and sacrifices legitimate suspense for pedestrian clarity. By the time of the composition of *A Midsummer Night's Dream* he has developed his sense of pace so well that the audience knows quickly what the state of affairs is and immediately becomes involved in the rapid progress of the developing action. Here the audience is provided with too much time in which to grow restive and indifferent as the playwright inexpertly tries to propel his action forward from a static beginning.

It has been justly remarked that:

He would have done all this in at most three scenes a few years later: one, as now, showing the planning of Julia with Lucetta to leave Verona and go to the court in search of Proteus; one preceding scene for Launce and Speed; and a longer scene, now scene 4 of Act II, in Milan at the Duke's palace, where the coming of Proteus to the court would bring out clearly his previous relations with Valentine and Julia, the love of Valentine for Silvia, the sudden infatuation of Proteus for her, and the place of Thurio in the story.[8]

[8]   George Baker, *The Development of Shakespeare as a Dramatist* (New York, 1923), pp. 118-119.

It is not until the play moves into Act III that there is any degree of suspense built up for the audience, Proteus' betrayal of Valentine to the Duke is used to set up the suspense-building scene where the rope-ladder is discovered and Valentine is banished.

Duke. Now, as thou art a gentleman of blood,
        Advise me where I may have such a ladder.
Val.   When would you use it? Pray, sir, tell me that?
Duke. This very night; for Love is like a child,
        That longs for everything that he can come by.
Val.   By seven o'clock I'll get you such a ladder.
Duke. But, hark thee; I will go to her alone.
        How shall I best convey the ladder thither?
Val.   It will be light, my lord, that you may bear it.
        Under a cloak that is of any length.
Duke. A cloak as long as thine will serve the turn?
Val.   Ay, my good lord.
Duke. Then let me see thy cloak.
        I'll get me one of such another length.
Val.   Why, any cloak will serve the turn, my lord.
Duke. How shall I fashion me to wear a cloak?
        I pray thee, let me feel thy cloak upon me.
        What letter is this same: What's here? "To Silvia"!
        And here an engine fit for my proceeding!

        . . . .

        Go base intruder! Overweening slave!
        And think my patience, more than thy desert,
        Is privilege for thy departure hence.   (III.i. 121-39; 157-60)

The treachery of Proteus in urging Valentine to flee Milan serves to heighten the dramatic impact of the scene. Furthermore the ensuing dialogue of Speed and Launce offers the audience an amusing parody of the romantic scene and affords relief from the dramatic tension until the dramatist is ready to build it up again. Launce's comment on the intrusion of Speed into the privacy of his love letter echoes the conflict between Valentine and Proteus and points to the course the resolution will follow:

Launce. Now will he be swinged for reading my letter, – an unmannerly slave, that will thrust himself into secrets! I'll after, to rejoice in the boy's correction.   (III.i. 392-395).

Here the playwright has used an effective dramatic sequence consisting of treachery, exposure, and banishment; and has counterpointed it by a scene of parody contrasting in tone with the main action but echoing it in content. Not only is this scene effective and amusing in itself; it also serves the purpose of propelling the action forward so that the audience will be concerned with the outcome of the perfidy of the faithless friend and the manner of his discovery. The main difficulty is that scenes like this are few and far between in this play. Furthermore, the expectations that are built up here are never sustained by subsequent scenes and the effectiveness of this climactic action is lost in the dramatic ineptitude of the resolution scene.

In the scene following the climactic rope-ladder scene, the action slows down to that of a transitional one, which it actually is, to prepare for the action that Proteus will now take in his intrigues against friendship, love, and social propriety. The general effect of this scene involving Proteus, the Duke, and Thurio is dramatically felicitous. The audience has seen the action rise to a crisis, been relieved of its tension through the use of comic contrast, and now it is being prepared to anticipate the subsequent action on the part of the main mover of the plot, Proteus.

The next act is dramatically uneven, being a mélange of sketchily handled scenes and skillfully handled vignettes. The first scene, showing the brigands capturing Valentine, has nothing to recommend it dramatically. It is inserted merely to serve the exigencies of the plot and to compensate for the playwright's lack of experience. It is neither fearsome so as to excite pity and fear, nor does it employ comic reversals so as to excite laughter. It is simply a contrived bit of action that provides the playwright with his needed blocking force. He needs this scene so that he can prepare for his resolution in which the audience may "rejoice at the boy's correction". The brigands could have been used to add to the comic tone by creating a *bomolochos* or *agroikos* (a refuser of the revels), among them to delight the audience with his buffoonish antics or churlish speech and also to serve as an active participant in the resolving action, but this he fails to do. They are all handled so inartistically, as is Valentine, that they become laughable in a way the dramatist probably never intended.

From the standpoint of plot mechanics scenes i and ii of Act III show definite evidence of a developing sense of stagecraft. From the standpoint of characterization and human interest, scene ii of Act IV is probably the best in the play. Here the action is built about the ironic situation of Julia, the love-lorn maiden, eavesdropping on a love-song sung by her lover but not to her. It is an effective scene not only because of the comic reversals in it but also because it serves to take Julia out of the category of mere "love-object" and place her in the category of "woman-in-love". This is an essential change that the playwright has to effect if he is ever to infuse life into the ethereal substance of romance. He is working toward a solution of the problem of motivation through characterization, and he is coming close to the answer. Besides being good in characterization, the scene is good in other respects also. For one thing, it helps to move the action forward another step. Since Julia now knows that Proteus is false to her, the audience can expect that something will result from this in the way of further complications and eventual resolution. The unfortunate part of all this is that the playwright does not use this auspicious characterization development to help him effect the dénouement. He creates the structure for what could prove to be an effective resolution, and then he simply abandons it in favor of resolution by accident.

After a short transitional scene in which Silvia is shown making preparations to escape from Milan in search of her banished lover, the audience is again provided with a scene in which Julia is further humanized toward the role of "woman-in-love" and away from that of mere "love-object" for the conventional lover of the *fine amor* tradition. (This scene is preceded by the humorously contrasting one in which the tone of romantic love is parodied in Launce's complete and abject devotion to his dog Crab who is forgiven and loved in spite of the foulest of offenses.) The delicate irony of this encounter scene between Julia and Silvia gives portents of better things to come in such plays as *Twelfth Night* where Olivia and Viola participate in a similar scene. It is not as deftly done here in this novice work nor as well sustained, but the playwright is not far from the dramatic desideratum of providing appropriate characterization as a necessary counterpart to an intricate plot.

But subsequent to this point the dramatist's lack of experience and foresight betrays him. Nothing he has done in the fourth act, aside from the insipid scene suggesting that Silvia is planning to run away, prepares for a resolution to the complications he has labored so hard to produce. It is now the burden of the fifth act to unravel this complicated knot, but it fails abysmally in its mission. The first scene is merely a weak repetition of something we already know. Showing Silvia in flight in company with the dramatically superfluous Sir Eglamour is closer to exposition, or at the most transition, than it is to dramatic action. The playwright is using it as a bridge to prepare for the cross-over from complication to resolution, but it is too fragile a structure to carry the weight of all the complications loaded on it. He needs something much more dramatic and suspense-building such as the discovery scene in Act III, but in a lower key. He might have used a change of garments between Julia, the supposed page, and Silvia thereby creating an ironic reversal of roles that might have led to an amusing scene of threatened rape instead of a stereotyped melodramatic one.

The second scene of this last act is also transitional, being used to show that the Duke and Sir Thurio have also left Milan, followed by Proteus and Julia, and can be expected to turn up where the playwright needs them in order to work out his resolution. A flimsy bit of action occurs in scene iii when Silvia is captured by the brigands with the superfluous Sir Eglamour nowhere in evidence. With two-thirds of his last act gone by, the playwright has only crudely structured the elements of his resolution. He has one scene left in which to effect a satisfactory and entertaining resolution. But it is in this vital scene that the dramatist exposes his greatest deficiencies of artistic technique: he cannot handle the resolution of the complicated plot he has constructed. He has shown he can develop and complicate his plot quite skillfully, but he cannot unravel his own tangled skein without resorting to the grossest of instruments and the most palpable of dodges. Later he will be able to handle this problem more skillfully, but in this apprentice effort, every character is stripped of any humanity that might have been developed in earlier scenes. Gone is the appeal that Julia had developed in the previous act: she takes no active part in the scene, her only contribution being an anguished sigh and a swoon. Proteus is not allowed to display any genuine emotion that might make his treachery understandable or his plea for pardon believable. Valentine is the mere walking shadow of courtly magnanimity, and Silvia reverts to being a mere "love-object" and loses any claim to redeeming femininity she might have shown promise of earlier in her scene with Julia. The scene is so poorly structured that it almost makes one forget everything of value that went before it: the suspense-building of Act III, the humanizing of Julia and Silvia in Act IV, and the intricate weaving of intrigue and ironic reversals. The playwright has forfeited all right to audience interest by a resolution scene that is too weak to be deserving of the name. Rather it should be called a "retreat" scene because the playwright abandons his forces on the field of battle with a hastily scribbled truce. Although he is aware of the value of a complicated plot and the necessity of creating suspense leading up to a single climactic action, he cannot yet proportion his early scenes to draw the audience into the action immediately, nor can he artistically resolve in his final scene the complications he has managed to contrive earlier. He has solved the problem of the middle of the play, but the proper handling of the beginning and end still requires much work.

As has been pointed out, much of his difficulty arises from the fact that he has not devoted enough attention to character development; nor does he use what characterization he has achieved to genuinely structural advantage. The work he does on Julia, Silvia, and Launce goes to waste since none of it is used to contribute to the resolution. Along with having Silvia and Julia exchange identities, he could have used Launce as a go-between to the supposed Silvia and perhaps have effected a resolution through the blunderings of the clown.

The other characters are so bound by the conventional limitations of romance that they never achieve any dramatic existence. Any life that Julia and Launce achieve arises from the fact that they are permitted to escape these limitations or lie outside them in the first place. If only Valentine or Proteus had been allowed to escape also, the dramatist could have used that character along with the other two to effect a dramatically satisfying resolution.

But, as it is, the weight of romance is too heavy, especially when the playwright does not use the very levers which he himself has created to move this inert mass of convention and idealism.

His levers consisted of characters like Julia and Launce, those outside the restrictions of romance. Although it is cause for disappointment that he does not fully exploit them in this play, they are reincarnated in later characters and serve their purposes admirably in other plays. In Viola and Rosalind character is allowed to motivate the complications and effect the resolution without so heavy a reliance on accident and convention as to mar the total effect of the play as occurs here.

Launce is as much out of his element in this conventionalized romance as is the womanly Julia. He has no real right to wander about in the fragile precincts of romance, but fortunately for the sake of humor in the play he has gained admission. He and Costard are elder brethren of the incomparable Bottom, the bell-ringer for the funeral of romance that takes itself too seriously. The defect is not in Launce, but in the limited use to which the playwright puts him. He uses his clown primarily for comic interludes, tentative parody, and messengerial functions in the main action. It is not until he creates Bottom that he realizes what a dramatic gem he has and really uses him as a clown should be used when he is part of a play. In this play, comedy is only interpolated with romance: it is not woven into its fabric as it later is in *A Midsummer Night's Dream*. Clownage and pantomiming are at their height with Launce and his shoe and his dog, but the laughter they occasion never spills over into the rest of the play.

In this present effort to create "romantic comedy" there is too much "romance" and not enough "comedy", at least not enough comedy which is produced by the main action. The playwright does not seem aware yet of the comic possibilities of the central action. He is handling it much too gingerly, as though it were too sacred to tamper with other than by complicating the action to build up intrigue and suspense. It is this attitude of respect, along with his incompetence in handling his exposition and resolution, that undoes his efforts. He has to learn to develop an attitude of irreverence toward lofty romantic ideals of love and friendship and see the absurdities inherent in the idealized excesses they are carried to in stories such as this one. The audience is asked to laugh and scoff at Sir Thurio and align itself with Valentine, but the laughter works in a perverse manner. Rather than Sir Thurio being the self-deluded one and therefore laughable, it is Valentine who is. For the playwright to ask the audience of a comedy to align itself with the deluded one is asking for a reversal of the traditional attitude. It can be done, as Cervantes proved later, but not with a character as conventionally drawn as Valentine. If Shakespeare had wanted us to laugh at Sir Thurio, he should have developed his pretenses as a pseudo-hero more and then exposed his true cowardice under a test as Jonson does with his gulls in *The Silent Woman*. We are asked to laugh at Sir Thurio because he is gullible and yet not possessed of any serious self-delusion as is Malvolio in *Twelfth Night*. He simply will not bear the burden of much laughter. All the laughter in the main situation, if there is any, will be directed toward Valentine and the absurd conventions he exemplifies, at least as far as a modern audience is concerned. The spirit of comedy is too closely allied to common sense to be on the side of impractical magnanimity and stereotyped valor. "Clearly, Shakespeare's first attempt to make romantic comedy had only succeeded so far that it had unexpectedly and inadvertently made romance comic."[9]

Even though characterization is inadequately developed and used and the action suffers from poor mechanics of exposition and resolution, the play might still have been salvaged by the use of the proper atmosphere and tone. For atmosphere he has selected the rarefied clime of Renaissance romance with geography and time distorted to fit the needs of the plot. One travels from Verona to Milan by a sea-voyage and banishment is followed immediately by the proclamation of a ducal edict, the posting of border guards, and the committal of the heroine to prison by her stern father, all occurring in the course of a soliloquy that requires but seventeen lines of text. But even these would not have been serious faults had other more important things been attended to. Had the atmosphere been that of sylvan enchantment softening the harshness of unpoetic reality, distortions of time and place would have been of no

[9]   Charlton, p. 43.

consequence. The playwright does not yet know how to call on the imagination of his audience; he strives for an air of verisimilitude but fails because his pretended reality is not real enough.

So also is the tone he creates inappropriate. Had the tone been that of amused tolerance of the extravagances and impossible idealism of youth he might have elicited gentle forgiving laughter from his audience at the all-too-human folly of his central characters. Had he been content to make them mere puppets controlled by supernatural urges beyond their control instead of people presumably motivated by rational considerations, he might have made them endearing because of their human helplessness. As it is he makes them unbelievable because of the incredibility of their motivations. Had he done all this, it would, of course, have been another play. And that is precisely what this play does become. It undergoes a thorough metamorphosis and becomes his later successes in romantic comedy: *A Midsummer Night's Dream* and *As You Like It*.

The geographic impossibilities and the temporal absurdities have nothing to do, then, with the real dramatic shortcomings of the play. It does not really matter for the purposes of comedy that Italy does not have inland waterways between Verona and Milan. If the connections within the character-action complex and within the atmosphere-tone complex are consistent and valid, one cares little about the connections between spots on a map. Cowled monks lurking in forests inhabited by quixotic bandits do not disturb the spectator either. What is disturbing is the failure on the part of the playwright to use the devices he has created to their best advantage. The outlaws could have been used as part of an atmospheric D plot as they later are in *As You Like It* or as sprites of the forest as in *A Midsummer Night's Dream*, but instead they are used as comic opera banditti who contribute to the action by a series of improbable accidents that render the action ludicrous rather than by fanciful inventiveness that enlivens the action. Their fault is that they are not corporeal enough and at the same time are too corporeal. Had one been able to poke a finger right through their seeming solid flesh, one might have been more content with their intervention. Had they been voices on the wind or music in the air, they would have served their purpose better, but the playwright is not emancipated enough from pseudo-reality to use out-and-out fantasy. He is inhibited by respect for a pseudo-reality which is farther from the truth of life than is pure fantsay. But he has poked his finger probingly into the ribs of these too corporeal denizens of the forest and is ready to turn them into intangible, airy nothings whose insubstantiality will do more for his plot structure than a mountain of flesh. These minions of Valentine are too cumbersome; they only appear to be facilitating action when actually they are stifling truly dramatic activity. With a theme as insubstantial as this, all pretense to reality must be abandoned; otherwise, one invites comparison by realistic standards which will destroy the credibility of the action portrayed. Puck and Ariel are more "natural" spirits of such a forest as this than are these *papier mâché* brigands of Shakespeare's Italy. But this one mistake has been enough; the next time the playwright knows how to handle the problem.

What would have helped to create the proper atmosphere, had the playwright been aware that this was one of the deficiencies of the play, would have been some degree of beauty of language to lift this whole "lamentable comedy" out of the realm of the prosaically romantic. But the language is rarely beautiful: there are scarcely a dozen lines worth repeating. The paucity of poetic language which characterizes this play can be seen in the images which dominate or, more properly, which fail to dominate the play and give it unity. The prevailing group of images is taken from types and classes of people without any apparent design. The dramatist uses similes involving the child, the babe, the nurse, the physician, the beggar, the pilgrim, the beadsman, the soldier, the swarthy Ethiope, the herald, the prisoner, the slave, the bastard, the messenger, etc. Julia, when she pretends lack of interest in Proteus' letter, says,

> Fie, fie, how wayward is this foolish love,
> That like a testy babe will scratch the nurse,
> And presently, all humbled, kiss the rod. (I.ii. 57-59)

In the rope-ladder scene, the Duke says,

> ... For love is like a child,
> That longs for everything that he can come by,
>
> (III.i. 124-125)

There is very likely no good reason why Shakespeare uses so many of this type of image in the play and why he repeats himself, as in the figures of speech involving the melting of a frozen or waxen image, except that he probably has no real sense yet of imagery being used to create and sustain tone and atmosphere. He may have written the play hurriedly and not have spent too much time on language.

For there is evidence, I think of haste of a kind we so rarely find in later plays, in the many repetitions of images, such as the comparison of the transitory nature of love by Proteus to the thawing of a waxen image, and by the duke to the melting of an ice figure; the references by both Proteus and Julia to 'Love's wings' and their swift flight, the comparison of the hardness of Julia's nature to steel, and of the dog Crab's to a 'pebble stone'; and the two uses of the chameleon, and of the spaniel.[10]

On the other hand, the playwright is beginning to use language to a more dramatic purpose – to develop character, as with Julia, and to build suspense, as in the rope-ladder scene between Valentine and the Duke – but he has gone too far along the road to pure utility and too far away from the paths of beauty and delight. This is the course opposite to the one he pursued in *Love's Labour's Lost*, and it must be considered only a qualified success. But he cannot abandon one element in favor of the other; he must learn to combine beauty and utility. Language must be used not only to develop character and to further action; it must also be used to create a suitable tone and atmosphere, to lend appeal through sound and imagery to all that happens in the play. Emotions must become lyrical, conflict must be charged with force of language, the soul of a character must hang suspended in his speech, and the poet must "give to airy nothingness a local habitation". All these must be done, but none of them are done with any great measure of success in this early effort. Up to this point in his development, when this playwright forsakes poetry, he abandons his chief asset. Recognizing his dramatic deficiencies, he has reacted so strongly to correct them that he lets his most natural talent fall into temporary discard. When he has

[10] Spurgeon, p. 268.

mastered the technique of plot manipulation and characterization, he returns to language and uses it to complement the mechanical aspects of playwrighting, thereby creating a unified effect.

Despite the marks of professional inexperience and possible haste, there are clear signs in the experimenting with complicated intrigues and multiple reversals that the playwright who was responsible for this near miss will not long continue to miss the mark: he will soon strike the target of romantic comedy in dead center. What he has to do now is to use the pattern of the A plot in *The Comedy of Errors* with the elements of the B plot from this play, with the latter parodied by a plot like the C plot in *Love's Labour's Lost*. To this must be added beauty of language and a D plot evolved from the outlaws of the forest of Milan. Once he does this, he will have the multi-level, tonally contrasting structure of *A Midsummer Night's Dream*, the next comedy he writes.

IV. *A MIDSUMMER NIGHT'S DREAM*

In studying the first three plays, the procedure had been to submit them to a detailed structural analysis in which attention was centered on the ironic reversals at the core of the various comic incidents. Consideration was given to how these reversals arose from changes of identity, character conflict, physical movement, and intrigue; how they were arranged climactically; and how the reversals in one plot tonally balanced or contrasted with those in other plots; and how one plot interacted with another in producing complications or resolution or in being complicated or resolved by another. Out of this study of sometimes tedious detail, there emerged what seemed to be a pattern toward which Shakespeare was moving. This pattern clearly involved a multi-level, tonally contrasting plot structure which was hinted at in the early comedies but never fully realized. By perceiving what was missing, one could see what would be created to fill the vacuum.

The study of this fourth selection – the play which first uses the full A-B-C-D structure – pursues a different method of investigation from that employed in the three earlier comedies. Instead of going into the minute analysis of incident and scene as before, the inquiry has been conducted on a more theoretical level, with the intention of summarizing what has gone before to induce general principles from the welter of fine detail – principles which would clarify the ideal structure of Shakespearean romantic comedy. Of necessity attention has been paid to certain pertinent details of this play, but such details are used primarily for illustration of the induced principles rather than as more raw data to be subjected to close analysis.

It was only through the pedestrian effort involved in the study of the earlier plays that material could be accumulated to support subsequent generalizations. The value of the previous, detailed study rests in great measure on the validity of the A-B-C-D structural formula which it led to and which exists in its ideal form in *A Midsummer Night's Dream* and only imperfectly in the three earlier comedies.

In these earlier works Shakespeare had imperfectly employed devices to create a diverse but unified effect which he never quite succeeded in achieving. Although he had learned to handle the core of the comic situation through the use of ironic reversals, to combine contrasting tones from different plots, to construct a parodying subplot structurally connected with the main plot, to use language brilliantly, and to raise story to its highest level of complication, he still had not achieved a satisfactory synthesis of all the elements he had mastered in one play. As soon as he had put one or two new elements into a play, he failed to put in elements he had handled successfully in a previous play. It was as though he was too uncertain of his powers yet to divide his attention among a wide range of complicated devices.

In *The Comedy of Errors* he had demonstrated he had the talent to handle the basic pattern of Plautine comedy with a high degree of success: he could handle rapid entrances and exits adeptly and could skillfully arrange ironic reversals in between which would lead to an ever increasing state of confusion. He had succeeded in creating a complicated comedy of situation, involving a clash of four actions, through the use of errors caused by a double shifting of identities. Out of his initial situation of doublets, he succeeded in creating an amusing series of complications and confusions involving ironic reversals of intention, of roles, and of fortune in a climactic pattern.

But successes on the level of mechanical manipulation of plot were counterbalanced by marked weaknesses elsewhere. For one thing, the tone of the work had been allowed to remain too long on the level of farce. He had, it is true, contrived an A plot, or enveloping action, with a contrasting, serious tone, but he had failed to intersperse with the main farcical tone contrasting notes from a parodying subplot (C plot) or from a complicating and resolving D plot. He had a rudimentary C plot in the antics involving Dromio of Syracuse and the kitchen maid, but the tone was identical with that of the main plot and the promised action of the C plot never developed beyond a mere episode which contributed nothing substantial to the structure of the play.

Furthermore, characterization had been shallow and mechanical, the principals in the action being borrowed mostly from Roman stage types with only minor modifications. The only genuine exception had been Luciana. Attempting to create a romantic heroine, he had spent some poetry in her characterization that would make her a woman, not just another blank-faced female necessitated by the exigencies of the plot. In Roman comedy the women were generally of two main types: the covetous courtesan who satisfied the physical desires of men and the shrewish wife whose affluence permitted the husband to philander but whose jealousy placed restrictions on him, with the ensuing complications and intrigues being the source of crude comedy. The young dramatist did not seem to have been satisfied with this oversimplified division. He was trying to create a female counterpart to the male comic protagonist who would have full dramatic equality with him. But the romantic heroine, beautiful in form and in soul, does not spring full-blown from the head of the playwright; she evolves slowly through several early attempts that never quite succeed. Luciana is the first of these, her attempted elevation occurring in the scene between her and Antipholus of Syracuse: he praises her beauty, but she gently upbraids him for his supposed infidelity to her sister. Although this is only an abortive attempt, in subsequent comedies he will spend more time and effort in creating this romantic heroine who will play a role dramatically equal to that of the male protagonist. In fact, she will even come to dominate the comedy, as Rosalind does in *As You Like It* or Viola in *Twelfth Night*. This attempt to elevate the romantic heroine to a role of dramatic equality with the male is not one which Shakespeare originated himself. He had probably observed its limited use by Greene and had been impressed by its possibilities enough to try it himself. At this stage of his development he lacked the skill to exploit it properly, but out of Greene's

Dorothea and his Margaret of Fressingfield no doubt came the germ of the idea for the more fully conceived heroines of Shakespeare's mature romantic comedy.

Another defect of his Roman effort which he soon strove to remedy was the absence of any truly multi-level action. The A plot, or enveloping action, was related to the B plot in a purely linear manner. The two plots intersected one another on the same plane and used the same timetrack: the events of the main plot occurred in between the events of the enveloping plot. The A plot was suspended, as it were, for almost three acts while the B plot was undergoing its complications and conflicts. Not till these complications and conflicts reached their climax did the A plot metronome start ticking again. This linear relationship of plots left too much to be desired. For one thing, it permitted the audience to lose awareness of a contrasting tone for too long a time. As a result of this time lapse, the total impact of the A plot would be dissipated by the time it emerged again, and the playwright would have to spend more time re-creating it. Time spent in this task would slow down the pace of the resolution in the B plot and hamper its effectiveness. What was needed was some kind of plot relationship involving several concurrent actions, any one of which could be brought to the foreground when the playwright saw fit to contrast tones and heighten impact. Plautine comedy had some of the static elements in the subordinate characters which would make this contrast possible, but the playwright did not yet know how to galvanize them into action independent of the main plot. The two slaves are used primarily as appendages to the main action; they do not have a separate C plot working to complicate or resolve the B plot or being worked on by some other plot. Whatever tone they add to the play is nothing but a reinforcement which the play definitely does not need. By accepting and adhering to the master-slave relationship of the Roman comedy, the English playwright had limited the dramatic possibilities open to him. He had not solved the problem of detaching the Dromios from the B plot and using them in their own space-time complex. This may appear to be a problem easy of solution, but this is true only because we can see how Shakespeare solved it in *A Midsummer Night's Dream*.

Actually, here again as with the elevation of the romantic heroine, he did not conceive the basic solution himself. The subplot was being used in Lyly's court comedy, and Shakespeare merely incorporated the device into his own plays and developed it further. But he not only imitated Lyly; he actually excelled him in the intricacy and subtlety with which he used this key device of the multi-level structure. It is easy to overlook the dramatic achievement entailed in handling a complex plot structure like that of *A Midsummer Night's Dream*, which ties in three or four separate lines of action so that they work independently yet influence one another and end in a common resolution. Even though Shakespeare did not himself originate the characterization device of elevation of the romantic heroine or the multi-level plot with contrasting tones, he did synthesize them into an organic complex which he employed with a high level of artistic excellence involving different variations of the basic pattern. He perfected the formula of the interlocking A-B-C-D plot structure and embellished it with a beauty of language and skill of characterization which has tended to obscure the real dramatic genius that went into the construction of his recognized triumphs in romantic comedy. Poetic touchstones have too often been used as the measure of Shakespeare's achievement. The real poetry of his accomplishment lies in the broader sense of the word: it exists in the artistic fashioning of the entire structure not just in the beautiful diction that is the most easily recognized feature of his greatness.

Despite its relatively barren language and lack of subtle characterization *The Comedy of Errors* has merit in that it taught Shakespeare that one of the secrets of the comic in life is the change of identities. Later on he learned that it did not have to be a physical change but could also be a change involving character. This is an important lesson; Henry A. Myers even considers it to be the basis of comedy, "The world of nonsense is ... governed by a law which is the exact opposite of the law of identity", which latter, he says, is the basis of the world of sense and order.[1] Shakespeare uses this principle as the basis of much of his comic structure. For example,

[1] *Tragedy: A View of Life* (Ithaca, 1956), p. 121.

in his last comedy, *The Tempest*, Trinculo and Caliban exchange their separate identities for that of a four-legged monster to the confusion of Stephano and to the delight of the audience. In *The Comedy of Errors* Shakespeare has effected this change of identities on the primitive level of a set of identical twins. In some plays he will use the physical device of disguise; in others he will use the more subtle device of characterization so that the comic figure changes identity from self-delusion, as Malvolio does in *Twelfth Night* or as Armado does in *Love's Labour's Lost*.

If we take stock of Shakespeare's progress at this stage of his development we can see what he has accomplished and what he still has to solve. He can now handle a B plot using ironic reversals based on physical changes of identity to produce laughter. He can combine two antithetical tones by contrasting that of his A plot with a dominant tone in the B plot. He can even interlock his A and B plots so that they effect complications or resolutions in the other. But for initial plot movement he has to rely on circumstances outside his main action. For complications within the B plot he leans very heavily on adventitious circumstance and coincidence. Characterization is stereotyped or, at best, rudimentary. Distinctions have been made between the characters of the two Antipholi, but they are scarcely of a critical sort. Both the courtesan and Adriana are basically stereotypes, and Luciana, like the mermaid that Antipholus of Syracuse compares her to, is only part human. As yet the playwright seems to have only the merest glimmer of a C plot and apparently not the faintest notion of a D plot, a plot which might help complicate and resolve the B or C plot and have its own conflict resolved by one of the other three plots.

Whether *The Comedy of Errors* preceded *Love's Labour's Lost* or followed it is of no real moment. Structural analysis would suggest that they both preceded *A Midsummer Night's Dream* even if there were no corroborating internal or external evidence. What the playwright was doing in these two plays was experimenting with two worlds of comedy. In the Roman play he had been concerned with the manipulation of incident as the basis of the comic. In *Love's Labour's Lost* he was experimenting with language, the parodying subplot, and theme as the basis of comedy. In the

Plautine comedy he had gone too far in the direction of mere mechanics; in the Lyly-inspired effort too far in the direction of quip and quibble and affected language in general. One of his strongest points – his mastery of poetic language – had become a dramatic liability here. He had permitted language to overshadow plot interest so much that the play might be considered a wasted effort structurally. What salvages it, however, is that he learned something basic about the multi-level plot structure, something that *The Comedy of Errors* shows little evidence of. In this court comedy he was learning to develop the C plot and use it to affect the action in the other plots and lend a contrasting tone. Paradoxically, however, he did not use the A plot as fully and successfully as he had in the Roman comedy. Here also the A plot was used to initiate the main conflict in the B plot, but the return of the A plot in the form of Mercade strikes one as an inartistic intrusion rather than as a careful, if somewhat obviously arranged, convergence of events as did that involving Aegeon and his two lost sons. Shakespeare seemed to sense that he needed an A plot to contrast with the tone of affectation and frivolity of the main plot, but in the attempt to import into the play the tone of natural events and serious concerns, he jars the audience into an awakening it is too unprepared for after the prolonged war of words. The tonal effect of Mercade's arrival serves to dispel rather than to create the illusion of organic unity.

But he did use the principle of complicating the B plot by intrusion from another plot in the device of the misdirected letters entrusted to Costard, the rustic comic in the C plot. Although the device effecting this interaction was a crude one, multi-level action was achieved. For the concept of the parodying subplot he was indebted to Lyly, but for the clever reversals within it he was probably indebted to no one but himself and his own ingenuity. In the Armado-Jaquenetta-Costard triangle we can see the plan for later parodying subplots. Although Holofernes and Nathaniel are not so successfully employed, they participate in an activity which reaches its zenith in the play-within-a-play section of the C plot in *A Midsummer Night's Dream*.

The structural problem in *Love's Labour's Lost* is not so much with the C plot as it is with the B, or main, plot. The playwright does not yet transfer what he has learned from classical comedy to a play of his own contriving. He does not seem particularly adept at complicating a story of his own devising. He seems to need a play, a story, or several stories, already cast, to manipulate to suit his dramatic intentions and theme. He as yet cannot create out of whole cloth without producing a rather flimsy garment. He has tried to arrange his incidents as Plautus had shown him could be done so that suspense is built up toward a climactic action which is followed by a swiftly executed, but not hastily contrived, resolution. But in *Love's Labour's Lost* he fails to achieve this sense of pace: there is very little dramatic suspense and a *deus ex machina* instead of a functional resolution. He strings his incidents together loosely and has to summon help surreptitiously in the form of Mercade to extricate himself from a dramatic impasse. Somehow he will have to contrive a way by which the Mercades are built into the play long before they are needed so that their appearance to resolve the complications will seem to be a plausible and even an inevitable occurrence, one which the audience can take intellectual delight in anticipating.

Up to this point, Shakespeare had successfully adapted a classical comedy and written a play of his own out of topical material and a popular courtly theme. Next he turned to an already existent story, discarded its dramatic irrelevancies, heightened its effect by selection and emphasis, and combined elements from other sources to add complexity to the plot and to fit the story to the requirements of his theme. *The Two Gentlemen of Verona* was the first comedy in which he employed this technique. Adapting a long, rambling piece of narrative fiction to the comic stage proved to be a much more formidable task than simply reworking an old comedy or concocting a bit of verbal fluff about the conflict between Love and Learning. He did not have the stagecraft of Plautus nor the artifice of Lyly to help him here. All he had was the leisurely action of a Spanish pastoral, the lessons he had learned from previous efforts, and his own ingenuity. He had to select, omit, emphasize, and combine all on his own. Although he did not fully succeed, he did add to his grasp of structure in the process.

He learned to take a loose narrative and turn it into a complicated B plot full of intrigue and ironic reversals. He even learned how to build up complications of his own devising to a suspenseful climactic reversal.

But he still had not made much progress with motivation. Neither Plautus nor Lyly had been of much assistance here. Not yet being able to motivate through the agency of characterization, and eschewing the too overt use of circumstance and accident, he relied heavily on moving his characters like pieces on a chessboard, putting them where he needed them to complicate the action, to engage in intrigue, or to bring about the resolution. To compensate for the shortcomings of this method, he experimented with three-dimensional characterization. Following the tack he had briefly pursued with Luciana in *The Comedy of Errors*, he worked on the characterization of Julia. The amazing thing about it is that he succeeded so well and yet still failed to use what he had achieved for motivational purposes. The importance of the achievement in three-dimensional characterization, however, overshadows his failure to exploit it fully. The device was there to be used and perfected in subsequent efforts.

In his effort to arrange the events in the B plot and to strengthen characterization techniques he temporarily ignored the principle of multi-level action which he had worked on in *Love's Labour's Lost* and reverted to the linear formula of *The Comedy of Errors*. Launce and Speed are cleverer and more entertaining than the two Dromios, but they do not participate in any more C plot than did these predecessors and in considerably less of a plot than did Costard, Armado, and Jaquenetta. They are still appended to the main plot as servants and are shackled by this relationship and by the playwright's preoccupation with other matters.

In his concern with complicating the B plot, he even neglected his earlier device of the tonally contrasting A plot. He carelessly incorporated what might have been an enveloping action involving the fathers of Valentine and Proteus into his exposition and thereby lost any function that he might have put it to in balancing his tones and establishing a point of reference for the action in his B plot. In order to go two steps forward in the B plot, the novice was forced to retrench in other areas to the detriment of the play considered in its entirety, but to the advantage of his developing skill as a complicator of plots and a creator of character. But such retrenchments are not true defeats; they are simply necessary mistakes in the course of a difficult apprenticeship. Shakespeare cannot use all of his skills to best advantage yet, but he is learning his trade and will soon have the craft completely mastered. Once this is done, he will know exactly how to use all the different elements.

There is still another large area of weakness left in his technique: he still does not know much about atmosphere or dramatic climate as an influencing factor in structure. In *The Two Gentlemen* he had embarked on his efforts under the wrong atmospheric conditions. He had chosen the apparently amenable atmosphere of Renaissance romance, but it had proved refractory. Under its influence, dramatic logic wilted, and characters swooned in its languid breezes. Unfortunately, this influence hurt his most viable characters and destroyed their potential usefulness. At this impasse, he knew he must find an atmosphere more congenial to the blend of romance and comedy than that provided by the forest of Milan.

Although he did not have the appropriate motivating atmosphere here, he did have the germ of the D plot, something he had shown no signs of creating earlier. The outlaws were only puny participants in an undeveloped D plot, but they provided the blocking force needed to bring about the resolution of the complications in the B plot.

It was not until he worked his way through the preceding plays and had become aware of the problem of combining all the separate skills he had mastered that he embodied in one effort all that he has learned about tonal contrast, multi-level plot, functional characterization, and motivating atmosphere. He was now ready to put into practice the complete pattern of romantic comedy that he had evolved by experimentation with the assorted materials of Roman farce, court comedy, and Renaissance romance. He was now ready to attempt a romantic comedy built around the multi-level plot with the interlocked and coterminous A-B-C-D plots which complicate and resolve one another and produce a single, harmonious effect by the combining of balancing and contrasting elements of tone character, and incident. He had learned how to combine tones ranging from the sentimental to the farcical. He no longer had to rely on mere chance and motivating circumstance outside the plot to provide impetus for the complications and intrigues of comic conflict: he can create character that is capable of propelling the action forward with a minimum of circumstantial intervention, and he can summon up atmosphere with the magic of his poetry which will help toward the same end. But all of this he owes to his comparative "failures" or, perhaps more accurately, limited successes in comic drama.

But the last play in this study is by no means a limited success; on the contrary, by the structural criteria established here, it is an unqualified triumph. The plot structure of *A Midsummer Night's Dream* is intricately multi-level, having four different elements: a serious, enveloping action; a romantic but comic one; a tonally contrasting, anti-romantic parody; and a complicating and resolving one which lends a motivating atmosphere of enchantment to the internal action through the agency of magical instruments.

Although the first printing of this play did not take place until 1600, when the First Quarto appeared, there is little doubt that the play was written at least five years earlier and no doubt that it was written before 1598 since Meres mentions it in his list. It is almost universally agreed that it was composed to celebrate some important wedding of the Elizabethan nobility. The Theseus-Hippolyta nuptials as the framework and limiting agency of the play and the elaborate masque-like use of song and dance strongly indicate such a possibility. Obvious compliments to the Queen in Oberon's "mermaid on a dolphin" speech would suggest that Elizabeth may have been present at the first showing. The most acceptable event to fit such a description would be the wedding of the Earl of Derby to Elizabeth Vere at the court in Greenwich in January 1595. Other bits of evidence such as Titania's speech on the inclement weather caused by Oberon's distemper and the Athenian mechanicals fear of "affrighting the ladies" with too fierce an impersonation of a lion tend to support this event and date. Such a likelihood as this 1595 date would fit in exactly with the dating of the play by structural surmises. A date such as January 1595 would place this play later than all three of the other comedies considered here, a supposition which is certainly indisputable on technical grounds, assuming this play did not undergo extensive revision later, a possibility which is generally not much credited.

The composite structure of the play is Shakespeare's own creation although most of the individual elements within it come from other sources. The idea for the opening situation of the play may have come from the first twelve lines or so of Chaucer's *Knight's Tale*. The character of Theseus may have been expanded by suggestions from Plutarch's treatment of him and Romulus. Ovid's *Metamorphoses*, probably through Golding's English translation in fourteeners, was the main source for the tale of the tragic lovers, Pyramus and Thisbe. The suggestion for the use of the Fairies may have come from previous plays such as *James the Fourth* by Greene, in which Oberon, King of the Fairies, appears. Folklore also played a part in their creation, especially in the case of Robin Goodfellow, whom Shakespeare named "Puck". The use of the Fairies and Midsummer's Day as part of the setting permitted the playwright to incorporate fantasy and magic into the structure of the play. Shakespeare even borrowed from himself: Bottom and his fellow actors trace their ancestry to Costard and the other Worthies of *Love's Labour's Lost*: the pairs of lovers are clearly related to those of the *Two Gentlemen*; and the farcical horse-play harks back to squabbles in *The Comedy of Errors*.

The most important borrowing from himself, however, occurs in the numerous structural devices developed in earlier plays which he employs here in a completely coordinated A-B-C-D multi-level structure. The characters and central incident of the enveloping action (the A plot), involving the impending nuptials of Theseus and Hippolyta, serve as the occasion for the introduction and exposition of the conflicts in the B plot revolving around the perversities of affection which are resolved eventually into two reciprocal loves. The first complication in the main action of Plot B occurs through the intervention of the main mover in Plot A, Duke Theseus, in the affairs of the Athenian lovers. The *senex*, Egeus, acts as the link between plots A and B where he serves as a blocking force to set up the basic conflict and then later acts as the endorser of the incorporation of Plot B into A following the resolution of the former.

When the four young people first appear on the stage, a situation of perverse affection already exists. For some reason outside the purview of the plot proper, Demetrius, who had earlier loved Helena, has transferred his love to Hermia who is already loved by Lysander and who reciprocates his love.

> *Lys.* I am beloved of beauteous Hermia.
> Why should not I then prosecute my right?
> Demetrius, I'll avouch it to his head,
> Made love to Nedar's daughter, Helena,
> And won her soul, and she, sweet lady, dotes,
> Devoutly dotes, dotes in idolatry.
> Upon this spotted and inconstant man.   (I.i. 104-110)

Helen then, although forsaken, still loves Demetrius and wishes to win back his affection, but the blocking force, Egeus, stands in the way of this possibility because he has successfully petitioned the Duke to authorize the marriage of Demetrius to his daughter, Hermia.

> *The.* For you, fair Hermia, look you arm yourself
> To fit your fancies to your father's will,
> Or else the law of Athens yields you up –
> Which by no means we may extenuate –
> To death, or to a vow of single life.   (I.i. 116-121)

This first internal complication in the B plot leads to triple intrigue just as the journey of Proteus to Milan led to a triple intrigue in *The Two Gentlemen.* Here it starts with Lysander's and Hermia's intrigue against society in their deciding to steal away to the wood that night to escape the edict of Duke Theseus. Helena, who is informed of the proposed flight in her role as friend and confidante to Hermia, intrigues against friendship by informing Demetrius of their plans. She engages in a further intrigue, this time against love, by chasing after Demetrius who is in pursuit of Lysander and Hermia.

This complication and intrigue in Plot B, which was initiated by action in Plot A, takes the characters of Plot B into the moon-bathed woods of Athens supervised by Oberon acting through Puck and the magical flowers, the main agents of Plot D, along with Titania.

Next, the characters and situation of Plot C, the Athenian mechanicals and their crude theatrical, are brought into the structure. Unlike the Dromios and the clowns of *The Two Gentlemen*, they are not mere appendages of the participants in either Plot A or B; their only connection with them is an indirect one in their role of citizens of Athens. Being thus emancipated socially, they are equally emancipated dramatically and therefore can carry on their own separate activities. These activities, centering around their rehearsal in the woods, form part of a complication converging on a conflict in Plot D. When that amiable ass, Bottom, becomes literally converted into an ass by the magic of the woods, he, in conjunction with the love-in-idleness flower helps to resolve the comic conflict between Oberon and Titania when the former takes pity on his poor queen for being enamoured of such an ass.

The initial movement of the characters in the C, or parody, plot takes them to the woods to rehearse the production of their amateur theatrical. This movement brings them into contact with the sphere of activity of the participants in Plot D. While in the woods, Bottom and his colleagues still remain independent of the participants in Plot B and A until after the reslotuion of the conflict in B and its incorporation into the A plot. The events of Plot C are not linearly connected with those of Plot B at this time, but are coterminous with them, a device useful for the creation of suspense since it permits the playwright to suspend immediate audience satisfaction by moving from one level of action to another.

The participants and situation in Plot D form a vortex toward which the lines of action of Plots B and C converge. Titania's doting on the little Indian boy operates as the pre-existing motive circumstance which provides the basis for Oberon's action. By his intrigue against Titania he is drawn into intervention in the affairs of Plot B. Actually, from a structural standpoint, his intervention in Plot B is the reason for his presence in the play, but Shakespeare has now learned how to convert a necessity into a virtue. Oberon is a resolving agent, like the outlaws and Mercade were, but he is not used inexpertly as they were. The playwright uses him not only to resolve the B plot but also in a plot of his own which is amusing in its own right and which heightens the amusement in the C plot. This device, simple on the surface, of a Fairy King at odds with his queen and seeking to resolve his conflict, but in the process creating and resolving complications in other plots is a master-stroke of dramatic invention. Lesser efforts in the use of resolving agents that went before culminate in this one brilliant flourish, one which the playwright continues to use to the very end of his career in the actions of Ariel seeking to gain his freedom and, by so doing, affecting the action of the C plot of Caliban, Stephano, and Trinculo and that of the B plot involving Ferdinand and Miranda.

This search on the part of Oberon for a solution to the conflict in Plot D leads to the second complication in Plot B. When Puck squeezes his magic juice on the eyes of Lysander, who awakens to be smitten by Helena, we get a "quadrangular duel of perverse affection".[2] Lysander is now in love with Helena; Helena is still in love with Demetrius; Demetrius with Hermia; and Hermia with Lysander. Each person is in love with exactly the wrong one from the standpoint of the loved one. What complicates the comic incongruity is the second reversal of intention that Oberon suffers. In attempting to rectify the perverse quadrangle of love, he squeezes the potent love-juice on the eyes of the right young Athenian, but at the wrong time, and succeeds only in reversing the situation that prevailed when the lovers first entered the wood. Instead of both young men pursuing Hermia in loving adoration as they did when they entered the magic forest, they are now both pursuing Helena, and it is Hermia who is the forlorn one. This reversal of roles on the part of the two young ladies leads to comedy on the farcical level when the skeptical Helena accuses them all of mockery and turns upon her friend from childhood who, in Helena's distressed mind, has changed her identity from friend to foe.

[2]   Moulton, p. 229.

> *Hel.* Lo, she is one of this confederacy!
> Now I have perceived they have conjoin'd all three
> To fashion this false sport, in spite of me.
> Injurious Hermia! Most ungrateful maid!
> Have you conspired, have you with these contrived
> To bait me with this foul derision? (III.ii. 192-197)

The broad comedy of vituperation and the pulling of hair results with the polite young ladies changing into brawling fishwives.

> *Hel.* Oh, when she's angry, she is keen and shrewd!
> She was a vixen when she went to school,
> And though she be but little, she is fierce.
> *Her.* Little again! Nothering but low and little!
> Why will you suffer her to flout me thus?
> Let me come to her. (III.ii. 322-328)

In the meantime, Plot C becomes entangled with Plot D when the rude mechanicals remove themselves to the Athenian wood to rehearse their "lamentable comedy" under the direction of the pacific Quince and with the indispensable services of the versatile Bottom, that master in the art of changes of identity. He can assume any identity required but paradoxically remains his own inimitable self throughout. The presence of this ass among men in the Athenian wood is sufficient to suggest immediately to Puck the solution of the conflict between Oberon and Titania: transfer her affection from the little Indian boy Oberon covets to this very opposite of a desirable love object for a fairy queen and the conflict is resolved. The only difficulty is that it comes off too successfully; the irrepressible Bottom accepts it with too much aplomb. He is constitutionally incapable of being nonplussed. Not even Oberon, the one who has profited directly from this incongruous infatuation, can permit such a union as that between the delicate Queen of Fairyland and the Prince of Asses, Master Nick Bottom. Bottom, with his literal-minded triumph over all the hazards of fate, is too much to inflict on Titania. Thus, by virtue of being what he is, that is, through characterization, Bottom becomes the resolving agent for Plot D and restores amity between Oberon and Titania; out of pity Oberon must release her from her dotage to this incredible ass and reconcile himself to her.

The D plot has been resolved, but the B plot is still in a state of chaos. With Demetrius and Lysander both having undergone a reversal of roles into lovers of Helena and the friendship between the two girls ruptured, things have gone as far as they can without undergoing repetitive complications and comically flat reversals. Things have come to an impasse and must now be resolved. Just as the D plot with its motivating atmosphere and magical agencies complicated the action of Plot B and turned things topsy-turvy, it must now set them right as was originally planned by Oberon before he suffered his reversals of intention. All that needs to be done to set them right is to disenchant the right young man. This is accomplished by the dropping of the juice of Dian's bud into Lysander's eye before he awakens and sees Hermia. Once done, the situation of quadrangular perversity in love is converted into one of harmony with two pairs of lovers and a four-way friendship.

The B plot is now ready for incorporation in the A plot: this is accomplished by bringing a hunting party composed of the characters in the A plot into the wood at daybreak, a time when the spell of enchantment has disappeared. When Theseus finds the lovers have solved their dilemma themselves, he pronounces the ritual of incorporation,

> Fair lovers, you are fortunately met.
> Of this discourse we more will hear anon.
> Egeus, I will overbear your will,
> For in the temple, by and by, with us
> These couples shall eternally be knit.   (IV.i. 181-185)

The complication in Plot C, the fact that the amateur theatrical group had lost its star performer, is resolved by the solution of the conflict in Plot D between Oberon and Titania. Once the King and Queen of the enchanted wood are reconciled, the garment of magic is removed from the shoulders of mortals and Bottom returns to the world of figurative asses so befuddled by the memory of his "translation" that he can only philosophize,

I have had a most rare vision, I have had a dream past the wit of man to say what dream it was. Man is but an ass if he go about to expound this dream. Methought I was – there is no man can tell what. Methought I was – and methought I had – but man is but a patched fool if he will offer to say what methought I had. The eye of man hath not heard, the

ear of man hath not seen, man's hand is not able to taste, his tongue to
conceive, nor his heart to report, what my dream was. (IV.i. 209-218)

Bottom is triumphant to the end; he knows the limitations of
human intellect and sense perception and he is not going to make
the mistake of trying to transcend them. Magic may change what
appears above his shoulders, but he is a creature of solid instinct
to his very bottom.

All that remains for the incorporation of the resolved C plot into
the A-B complex is to permit them to come into contact. With the
coming of the dawn, the symbolic end of the rule of fantasy and
magic, events move back into the world of common sense and law
and order, the world of Theseus, where things do not change their
identities momentarily and where one can predict human behavior.
Now that the initial complication arising outside the play that had
caused the original triangle of perverse affection has been resolved
by contact of the world of irrational human passion with the world
of fancy and imagination, no true conflict exists any longer.
Passage through the world of imagination and poetic fancy has
converted irrational passion into controlled desire so that it can
now be admitted to the world of reason and common sense.
The eyes of sane judgment as exemplified by Theseus can recognize
this transformation and realize that the established order is no
longer threatened by passion that runs riot, knowing no restraint of
custom or of reason. Egeus would cling to his ritualistic objections,
but now his remonstrances are no longer worthy of serious attention
and instead would become ludicrous if he persisted in them. Common sense is now on the side of the lovers, and Egeus is silenced by
the logic of events. There are no longer any obstacles to the course
of true love; they have been removed by the magic hand of imagination, and their removal has been attested to by the guardian of
reason, Duke Theseus.

The conjoined A-B society temporarily resists the inclusion of the
participants of plot C into its newly unified structure. But through
the tolerance of the prime mover of plot A, who has already accepted the participants of plot B (the representatives of the role of
passion in human life), the participants of plot C (the representatives
of the role of instinct in human life), are also accepted,

> *The.* I will hear that play,
> For never anything can be amiss,
> When simpleness and duty tender it. (V.i. 81-83)

Thus along with reason and controlled passion in the life of man, we have the necessity of "simpleness" or instinct recognized. A balanced society now exists, composed of the reconciled contrasts between reason and passion and the rescinded exclusion of instinct. The influence of fantasy and imagination hovers in the background, but its effect is beneficent when reason is in charge of the other levels of human nature. Reason is immune to the disruptive influence of fantasy; human passion, under the aegis of reason, can work its way through to controlled desire; and earth-bound instinct will paradoxically rise above the highest flights of fantasy in the literal-minded triumph of Bottom over magic.

In terms of structure, plot D is not incorporated into the A-B-C complex but remains as a distinct entity. It does, however, take its farewell in the form of a song and dance, the agents of its power that are left behind in the world of common sense, controlled passion, and instinct as reminders of its potential influence in human affairs.

Thus, it can be seen how the playwright has learned to incorporate meaning into structure. He no longer needs to rely on such artificial themes as Love versus Learning or Love versus Friendship, engrafted on a plot and determining its actions to the detriment of structure, in order to convey meaning. Nor does he have to employ explicit statements of his theme through the use of a spokesman in the play to express his reflections on life. The meaning of the play now rises out of its structure. But the total impact is not merely an intellectual one; the insight goes deeper than that, involving a total response on the part of the audience – calling on intellect, emotion, instinct, and fancy. With such a structure the meaning of comedy approaches the profundity of tragedy. Its levity is profundity in another direction; it simply involves a different view of life based on the recognition of compromise in human affairs, something which the tragic protagonist refuses to admit into his scheme of things.

This study was undertaken with the hope that it might provide a greater degree of insight into Shakespeare's methods and dramatic development in the writing of comedy. It was hoped that the study might lead to a better understanding of the mechanics of the plays – why certain things were done at a certain time, why characters were drawn as they were, and why the particular setting was chosen. It was further hoped that the study might provide criteria to determine how effectively Shakespeare had combined the dramatic elements he was employing – where he had fallen short, and where he had hit the mark. Finally, it was hoped that it might illuminate the way in which structure could be used to shape meaning, how Shakespeare expressed his view of the world through the incidents, characters, and tone he created and the attitude he demonstrated toward them.

The major conclusion arrived at from this inquiry is that Shakespeare, by means of a multi-level, tonally contrasting A-B-C-D structure, which he created out of elements borrowed mainly from others, devised an effective dramatic means of combining high entertainment with deep insight into the human condition, a goal in art held in the highest esteem since classical antiquity. Through the use of this method he captured the spirit of classical art without resorting to the formalism appropriate to another age but not to his own day. This study would suggest that his genius lies not alone in his poetry, great as it is, but in this development of a comic structure suited not only to the tastes of an Elizabethan audience but also to the tastes of all who look for unity in diversity and entertainment coupled with insight in a work of art.

BIBLIOGRAPHY

Baker, George, *The Development of Shakespeare as a Dramatist* (New York, 1923).

Baldwin, T. W., *William Shakespere's Five-Act Structure* (Urbana, 1947).

Bergson, Henri, "Laughter", in Wylie Sypher (ed.), *Comedy* (New York, 1956).

Boas, Frederick S., *Shakespeare and his Predecessors* (New York, 1905).

Bradbrook, Muriel, *The Growth and Structure of Elizabethan Comedy* (London, 1955).

Bullough, Geoffrey, *Narrative and Dramatic Sources of Shakespeare* (London, 1957).

Chambers, E. K., *William Shakespeare* (London, 1924).

Charlton, H. B., *Shakespearian Comedy* (New York, 1938).

Clark, Eva Turner, *The Satirical Comedy "Love's Labour's Lost"* (New York, 1933).

Craig, Hardin, *An Interpretation of Shakespeare* (New York, 1948).

Frye, Northrup, *The Anatomy of Criticism* (Princeton, 1959).

Goddard, H. C., *The Meaning of Shakespeare* (Chicago, 1951).

Hughes, Leo, *A Century of English Farce* (Princeton, 1956).

Lyly, John, *The Complete Works of John Lyly*, ed. R. W. Bond, 2 vols. (Oxford, 1902).

Meader, William, *Courtship in Shakespeare* (New York, 1954).

Moulton, Richard G., *The Moral System of Shakespeare* (New York, 1907).

Muir, Kenneth, *Shakespeare's Sources* (London, 1957).

Myers, Henry A., *Tragedy: A View of Life* (Ithaca, 1956).

Nicoll, Allardyce, *Shakespeare: An Introduction* (New York, 1952).

Pollard, A. W., *Shakespeare's Fight with the Pirates* (Cambridge, 1920).

Shakespeare, William, *Love's Labour's Lost*, ed. Wilbur Cross and Tucker Brooke (New Haven, 1925).

——, *Love's Labour's Lost*, ed. Sir Arthur Quiller-Couch and John Dover Wilson (Cambridge, 1923).

——, *The Complete Plays and Poems of William Shakespeare*, ed. William Allen Neilson and Charles Jarvis Hill (Cambridge, 1942).

Spurgeon, Caroline, *Shakespeare's Imagery and What It Tells Us* (Cambridge, 1935).

Thomas, Sidney, "The Date of *The Comedy of Errors*", *Shakespeare Quarterly*, Autumn, 1956, pp. 376-384.

Yates, Frances A., *A Study of "Love's Labour's Lost"* (Cambridge, 1936).

STUDIES IN ENGLISH LITERATURE

Out:

1. WILLIAM H. MATCHETT: *The Phoenix and the Turtle. Shakespeare's Poem and Chester's Loues Martyr.* 1965. 213 pp. Cloth. Gld. 26.—

2. RONALD DAVID EMMA: *Milton's Grammar.* 1964. 164 pp. Gld. 18.—

3. GEORGE A. PANICHAS: *Adventure in Consciousness. The Meaning of D. H. Lawrence's Religious Quest.* 1964. 225 pp., portrait. Gld. 25.—

4. HENRIETTA TEN HARMSEL: *Jane Austen. A study in Fictional Conventions.* 1964. 206 pp. Gld. 25.—

5. DOROTHY SCHUCHMAN MCCOY: *Tradition and Convention. A Study of Periphrasis in English Pastoral Poetry from 1556-1715.* 1965. 289 pp. Gld. 30.—

6. TED E. BOYLE: *Symbol and Meaning in the Fiction of Joseph Conrad.* 1965. 245 pp. Gld. 24.—

7. JOSEPHINE O'BRIEN SCHAEFER: *The Three-Fold Nature of Reality in the Novels of Virginia Woolf.* 1965. 210 pp. Gld. 24.—

8. GERARD ANTHONY PILECKI: *Shaw's "Geneva". A Critical Study of the Evolution of the Text in Relation to Shaw's Political Thought and Dramatic Practice.* 1965. 189 pp. Gld. 20.—

11. KENNETH HUGH BYRON: *The Pessimism of James Thomson (B.V.) in Relation to his Times.* 1965. 174 pp. Cloth. Gld. 20.—

18. EDWARD VASTA: *The Spiritual Basis of "Piers Plowman".* 1965. 143 pp. Cloth. Gld. 18.—

MOUTON & CO. — PUBLISHERS — THE HAGUE